Perceiving The Affordances

A Portrait of Two Psychologists

Perceiving The Affordances

A Portrait of Two Psychologists

Eleanor J. Gibson

2002

LAWRENCE ERLBAUM ASSOCIATES, PUBLISHERS

Mahwah, New Jersey   London

Lawrence Erlbaum Associates, Inc., Publishers
10 Industrial Avenue
Mahwah, NJ 07430

Cover design by Kathryn Houghtaling Lacey

Library of Congress Cataloging-in-Publication Data

Gibson, Eleanor Jack.
Perceiving the affordances : a portrait of two psychologists / Eleanor J.
Gibson
        p. cm.
Includes bibliographical references and index.
ISBN 0-8058-3949-6 (cloth : alk. paper)

BF109.G5 A3 2001
150'.92'2—dc21
[B]   2001023953
                                                      CIP

Books published by Lawrence Erlbaum Associates are printed on
acid-free paper, and their bindings are chosen for strength and durability.

Printed in the United States of America
10 9 8 7 6 5 4 3 2 1

Contents

Preface

My purpose in the following pages is to tell the story of a couple of scientists married to one another and working in much the same field. I want to show that it is possible to raise a family and do one's job (pretty well, in our case) without sacrificing one's independence. Yes, there were what some would consider sacrifices (when I gave up my safe teaching job at Smith for a completely uncertain research future), but with plenty of love, family support, and imagination it can turn out to be far more interesting than sticking to that safe spot. My husband and I both loved intellectual adventure, and it led to frequent travel, new friends, well-educated children, and most important, some new insights in science. There was the extra bonus of friends in many places and wonderful students.

In these chapters I have referred to my husband by more than one name; as James, Jimmy, Jim, and J. J., but never Professor Gibson. I called him Jimmy, his parents and brothers called him Jim, and his students called him J. J. Despite these familiar appellations, I refer to him as James. That was his given name and it has dignity that I want to convey. I have had several names, too. To my parents and friends, as I grew up in Illinois, I was always Eleanor.

When I went to college, I was immediately dubbed Jackie (a popular kind of nickname at the time), and I have remained Jackie to most people. When I moved to Vermont in 1987, however, I returned to my original given name. The students, incidentally, referred to me as Mrs. G.

My text is a mixture of personal history, anecdotes, and intellectual auto-biography. I aimed for the intellectual autobiography, because I feel strongly that my husband's intellectual progression from the sensory-based, associative theory of perception (1929) to an ecologically oriented theory of perception (1979) all his own creation, needed to be put in a life setting, related as a story, and his persistent motivation shown. I also wanted to relate how I found a field of my own, perceptual learning, that eventually matured into an ecologically oriented theory of perceptual development including perceptual learning as an essential process. The anecdotes I have included are partly to satisfy my family and partly because I enjoy the recollections. They enliven the story a bit, too.

Who do I hope will read this book? Psychologists, of course, because I want them to be acquainted with the theories I recount, and to understand how they developed. I hope it will also be read by young professionals who are concerned about working out a life together with two careers.

1

Growing Up
in the Heartland

B oth James and Eleanor Gibson grew up in the Midwest, with its long vistas of plains and corn-fields as far as the eye could see. James Gibson had, indeed, occasional exposure to the grandeur of the far West, because his father was a railroad man and could take his family for vacations on train trips as a perquisite of his profession. But both were eager to escape to the East. First things first, however.

James Jerome Gibson was born on January 27, 1904, in McConnelsville, Ohio, at the home of his Grandmother Stanbery. His mother, née Mary Gertrude Stanbery, had previously had two stillborn infants, so this healthy son was cherished by his parents, grandmother, and a great aunt, Miss Mary Merriam, a tiny maiden lady. Both of these women later lived with the Gibson family. McConnelsville is a small town in southern Ohio on the Muskingum River near the farm of the Stanbery forebears where Gertrude Stanbery Gibson grew up. I happened, in an absurd way, to see the town once. There was a meeting in 1988 at Miami University in Oxford, Ohio, of the Society of Eco-

Opera House - 1890

Morgan County Courthouse - 1858

McConnelsville, Ohio

Birthplace of James J. Gibson (1904 - 1979)

Fig. 1. McConnelsville, Ohio; Birthplace of James J. Gibson, 1904–1979.

logical Psychologists, a group inaugurated after James's death by his followers. I was driven to the meeting by David Lee, an old friend and one-time student of James's from Edinburgh, Scotland. Accompanying us was Karen Adolph, a graduate student of mine dating from a sojourn at Emory University (she says David was driving her car). As we sped homeward from the meeting along a major turnpike, a crossroad appeared with a sign advising that McConnelsville was 30 miles to the south. David, spotting it, said, "McConnelsville! That's where Jimmy was born—let's go!" He slowed the car and turned south, despite Karen's and my protests that there was nothing to see. We arrived at the center of a small, old, respectable Midwestern town. "Where's the house?" asked David. I assured him that I had no idea and anyhow, it would have been his grandmother's house; he was only born there because his father was currently being moved to a new post by the Northwestern Railroad, where he served as right-of-way agent. David persisted and checked with a local historical society, but of course we never found the house. Several years later, after the story had made the rounds, I received a very large framed panoramic photograph of the center of McConnelsville, complete with courthouse, church, war memorial, and so on. Under the picture was an engraved title, "McConnelsville, Ohio; birthplace of James J. Gibson, 1904–1979". The photographer was Tom Stoffregen, my old graduate student, by then a professor at the University of Cincinnati, not far away from McConnelsville. The picture now hangs in the faculty room of the Psychology Department at Cornell University.

James was followed by two brothers, Thomas (Tom), born 4 years after James and William (Bill) born 4 years after Tom. Their father, who adored them, often pretended to confuse them, saying to one or the other, "Jim, Tom, Bill—whoever you are!" The family moved several times, living in Ohio, Wisconsin, and South Dakota before Thomas Sr. was finally assigned to Chicago for good. Then it was time for a permanent residence, and a house was built on 10th Street in Wilmette, Illinois, a middle-class suburb on Lake Michigan, north of Chicago. It was handy for commuting to the city on the Northwestern train, which stopped for passengers just a block north of the family residence, and connected with the "El" to The Loop, the Chicago business area where Thomas Sr. had his office.

The house was a rather large off-white stucco building with a front porch (everyone in Wilmette had a front porch), a sunroom in the back, and above the sunroom a sleeping porch that connected with one of the back bedrooms. This arrangement allowed the three boys to be housed in a single area, an advantage because both Grandmother Stanbery (Gertrude Gibson's mother) and her sister, Aunt Mary, came to live with them in Wilmette.

Aunt Mary was a little weak in the head and must have been a trial to her niece and nephew (a very patient man, however). Grandmother Stanbery, according to her grandsons, was a plus and often helped them with their math. She was also a wise and helpful counselor and babysitter, which was more than could be said of Aunt Mary, who once gave my son (age 2), her great-nephew, a large carving knife to play with.

Although there was an ample living room and a dining room, much of the family's time was spent in the sunroom. Most meals were served there on a two-piece walnut table that could be joined in the center. Half of the table is now cherished by Betty Gibson (Tom's wife) and the other half by my daughter Jean, Gertrude and Thomas Gibson's granddaughter. Five of the chairs (cherry with twisted spindle backs and cane seats) are at my son's house in South Carolina. Homework was done in the sunroom, and every Sunday afternoon, Thomas Gibson, treasurer of the First Presbyterian Church of Wilmette, spread the day's offering over the table as he sorted it, counted it, recorded it in an impressive ledger, and sealed it up for its trip to the bank. No one was ever allowed to help. The Gibsons and the Stanberys were founders of one of the earliest Presbyterian churches in Ohio.

James and his brothers grew up in Wilmette, attending a nearby school and never missing Sunday school at the church. We still have a Bible given to James for perfect attendance, with a note remarking on this by the minister. It is not exactly well worn, but the old leather binding is dry and cracked. The boys not only went diligently to Sunday school; they were also expected to work diligently (however reluctantly) in the large vegetable garden behind the house. The garden was productive, and vegetables were canned, jellies made, and so on, for Gertrude Gibson was a very thrifty housewife. She sewed, too, making clothes for herself and even for the boys as long as that was practical. I still remember her homemade Sunday dresses, not very stylish but very respectable. She had a favorite store in Chicago, Carson-Pirie & Scott, where she purchased sturdy, medium-priced clothing and dry goods.

The lake was a wonderful place to bathe and swim, with a sandy beach to play on. Gertrude Gibson did not swim herself, but she sometimes went there with the boys, to keep an eye on them. On one occasion, Tom swam out to a raft and stayed there a long time with companions, visibly shivering. The next day, Gertrude made the train trip in to Carson-Pirie's to buy herself a bathing suit so that she could better monitor the swimming activities. When she arrived home, Grandmother Stanbery met her at the door, saying, "Tom's sick—you'd better call the doctor." Tom had polio, which was epidemic at the time. He recovered, but had a game leg for the rest of his life.

Gertrude Gibson's social life was centered entirely in her church and in her family. This was her inclination, to be sure, but it was further ensured by her growing deafness. Before she was middle-aged she was totally dependent on a hearing aid, at the time a very awkward contraption with large batteries that had to be contained and hidden somewhere in one's dress. She was a cheerful, good-tempered person, nonetheless, and took her trial in her stride. The deafness was of genetic origin. She had one brother (referred to in the family as "Unc") who was also deaf. He lived in West Virginia and had something to do with oil wells. His wife must have died young, but he had one daughter, Virginia. They were only rarely heard from, but Gertrude also had two sisters, with whom she was always in close touch.

One sister, Eurie Stanbery, married Will Nichols, a dentist in Medina, Ohio. Gertrude always traveled to Medina for any dental work. The Nicholses had four children. The oldest, Abner, was a few years older than James Gibson, and became a chemist (later he was killed in an explosion at DuPont). Then came Ruth, Stanbery, and Ellen. All four of them graduated from Oberlin College and went on to further study. Gertrude's other sister, Maude, married Tom McCoy and lived in Twin Falls, Idaho. She had two sons. Neither of Gertrude's sisters was deaf, fortunately. They often visited back and forth.

Thomas Gibson, Sr., had three sisters, Jessie, Cad, and Mildred. Aunt Cad married and had one son, who died in his youth. Aunt Mildred never married, but became a very successful business-woman. Cad was widowed early and the two sisters lived together in Los Angeles. Jessie, the eldest sister, married "Uncle Link." They lived in southern California, too, and had a small holding where they grew oranges, walnuts, and the like. They had one daughter, Fern. Fern married and had a daughter, Jesslyn. Fern was widowed very early and Jesslyn was the spoiled darling of the whole California family, who were very close.

With all these relatives in the West and Midwest, the Gibson family traveled often, as Thomas Gibson's free passes on the Northwestern Railroad made the travel easy. However, Pullman berths had to be paid for and that was expensive for a family of five. I remember my mother-in-law explaining to me that she and her husband always shared a berth, which was quite tolerable if their heads were at opposite ends. The travel, in any case, was fun and educational for the boys. James wrote later that he got his first inkling of the importance of optical flow as information for the perception of distance from the rear observation platform of a train.

The schools in Wilmette were good. The boys attended New Trier High School, shared by three suburbs north of Chicago, known for its excellence throughout the Midwest. James Gibson was a reader and a good student. He was no athlete, but debated (with gusto and pleasure, I am sure, because he always loved an argument) and took part in high school dramatics. For some reason, the high school did not require 4 years of Latin, and when it came time to choose a college, James found that Princeton, his choice, would not admit him with only 2 years. Never mind, he took his freshman year at Northwestern University, and transferred as a sophomore to Princeton, which mysteriously forgave the lack of Latin after 1 year at another institution.

Eleanor Jack was born December 7, 1910, in Peoria, Illinois. Peoria is the second-largest city in Illinois, situated on the Illinois River, at the spot where the river widens into a large lake. The name (not to be scoffed at) means "beautiful view" in the language of the Indians who once inhabited the land. The land next to the river is flat, perhaps 2 miles wide on either side; above the flat land are tall bluffs from which the view is, in fact, very beautiful. The flat land was settled first, of course, and later gave way to businesses and manufacturing, as the bluffs were taken over for dwelling places. The location afforded excellent transportation on the river, and the city became a railroad hub as well. The Caterpillar Tractor Company settled there (on the "other" side of the river), and many other businesses, too. The Board of Trade (in the center of the best corn-producing land in the country) hummed with activity, especially before Prohibition.

My maternal grandmother's parents, the Clarkes, moved to Peoria from the East. My great-grandfather, Samuel Strong Clarke, originally a Connecticut Yankee, had been a successful importer in Charleston, South Carolina, but he found the climate unhealthful. In 1856 he moved his family to new land in Illinois where he expected to settle down as a gentleman farmer. He built a home, Cottonwood (still in existence), and planted not just the corn of the country but more exotic things, such as grapes from which wine was made. We still had Cottonwood wine on holidays when I was a child. He also founded a dry goods company (Clarke & Co). Two of his sons helped run it when they grew up. My Great-Grandmother Clarke, née Katherine Elizabeth Burns, came from New York City, where we think her father was a silversmith. She had a great deal of gorgeous silver, which the family still possesses. Her heritage was Scottish, so the family was Presbyterian and Great-Grandfather Clarke became one of the founders of the Second Presbyterian Church of Peoria (as did my Great-Grandfather Grier). The Clarke family was said to have been conveyed to Illinois from South Carolina in a coach lined with blue satin, which was later set on fire as a prank by the two younger sons. An apocryphal story, perhaps, but told in the family.

My maternal grandfather's parents were of Scotch–Irish ancestry and had moved west from Pennsylvania where the family originally settled. My grandfather's name was Thomas Atherton Grier, and his parents were considered (by my mother) very austere. They were Presbyterian too, of course, and Great-Grandfather Grier, as mentioned, was a cofounder of the Second Presbyterian Church. My grandfather had a brother Robert and a sister Anna (later Anna Jack). A cousin, John Grier Hibben, grew up with them. His mother, known as Cousin Jenny, was the widow of a Presbyterian minister and the Griers gave them a home. John Grier Hibben later became president of Princeton University. My grandfather became a corn broker on the Chicago Board of Trade.

My father's family also came to Illinois from Pennsylvania, again of Scotch–Irish stock and stout Presbyterians. My Great-Grandfather Joseph Jack was a general in the Civil War, serving in the Union army. We have a picture of him taken with his fellow officers in New Bern, North Carolina, in 1863. He moved west rather late in life, to Decatur, Illinois, where I had many Jack relatives, including my grandfather's two sisters, Aunt Anna Roberts and Aunt Elizabeth Wells, both tall and awe-inspiring ladies. My grandfather and his brother, my great-uncle William Jack, settled in Peoria; my grandfather, Francis Heron Jack, in the wholesale hardware business; and his brother as a lawyer. My great-uncle William married my great-aunt Anna Grier, so their children (four of them) were double cousins of my parents. All four of those children remained single and gave a lot of affection to my sister and me. One last word about the Jacks: My grandfather and his brother and sisters grew up in a large stone house in southwestern Pennsylvania that the family had inhabited for a century, near a village called Pleasant Unity. We have a picture of the house painted by my great-aunt Elizabeth from memory. The walls were so thick, she said, that three children could play at once in a window embrasure. The house still stands, now a country vacation home for a New York family.

My grandmother Jack died before my parents were married. Her name was Anna Kilgore (more Scotch–Irish). Her grandfather and his six sons all fought in the Revolutionary War, as did my great-great grandfather Jack as a very young man. (That was an unusual case of a father serving in the Revolutionary War and his own son in the Civil War.) My great-grandfather General Joseph Jack and his wife, Hanna Jane Heron Jack, had a 50th wedding anniversary in Decatur in 1892. All the grandchildren and a few other privileged children (including my mother) attended the celebration and each child presented the couple with a silver spoon with the date and the child's name engraved on it. I have one engraved Will (for my father) and my sister Emily has three; one says Isabel (my mother), one Emily (our father's sister), and the third, Hartley (for the son of a cousin, Jenny Jack Clarke; there was a lot of intermarriage in those days!).

My parents, of course, knew each other practically from birth, attending the same schools and Sunday school and having common relatives. My mother grew up in a double house (downtown) that held her family (her parents, older sister Caroline, younger brothers Tom Jr. and S. Clarke Grier, and two faithful servants, Emma and Tillie). There also lived the family of my great-uncle William Jack and Anna Grier Jack (my grandfather Grier's sister). They had four children, Robert, Sarah, William, and Elizabeth (Bess). Bess was exactly my mother's age and the two girls were inseparable, even through college. Both graduated from Smith College in 1903.

I knew less about my father's family because his mother, Anna Kilgore Jack, died so young. My father had two elder sisters, Emily and Jane, both very tall, handsome women, and a younger brother, Francis (named for his father, Francis Heron Jack). One of my father's legs had been severely injured in an accident as a child, and he limped for the rest of his life (it did not keep him from playing golf or going duck hunting, however). His name, William, was identical with one of his cousins. When he and my mother were married, my Grandmother Grier, his future mother-in-law, needed a middle name when she was ordering the wedding invitations. All she knew was A, which Dad used to distinguish himself from his cousin William Jack. Grandmother liked the sound of Alexander, which she ordered printed on the invitations. My father was known ever after as Bill Alec. By the time my parents married, all the families had moved up on the "Bluff" (the west bluff, preferred, for some reason to the east). They were married at home, with many Chicago Board of Trade friends of my grandfather's as guests, all of whom came through with expensive (fairly useless) wedding presents. My sister and I are still wondering what to do with some of them.

My parents settled in a modest middle-class home not far from my grandmother's house and just a few doors down the street from my Aunt Caroline. Aunt Carrie and Uncle Herbert Jamison had four children, Herbert Jr., Katherine (Cassie), and the twins Tommy and Mary, of whom one (Mary) was sickly and probably mildly epileptic. My cousin Cassie was just 1 year and 2 months older than I was, and we were close friends, sisters almost, always at one or the other's house. My own sister, Emily, was nearly 6 years younger than I, so Cassie and I, during childhood, were always closer.

We grew up in an extended family with many relatives. At Christmas and Thanksgiving dinners, always held at my Grandmother Grier's house, there had to be two tables and two turkeys. One table, set up in the large front hall, was the children's table. All the young cousins sat there together, monitored by my great-aunt (grandmother's sister), Isabel Clarke. She was very much a maiden lady, known to us children as Auntie Belle. She took care of her parents until they died and Cottonwood was sold. Then she lived for a while at my grandmother's home, but that didn't work. An arrangement was finally made for her to live with us (my mother was her namesake). A room was built on the back of the house (upstairs) for her. At the same time, a sunroom was added downstairs, with a sleeping porch above it; oddly enough, the same arrangement for extra space as my husband-to-be's house in Wilmette. Sleeping porches were considered wholesome for children, and were very cold in winter.

My cousin Cassie started grade school at 7 (almost; her birthday was in October). I was still only 5 (my sixth birthday not due until December); but my mother went to the hospital to produce my sister at that very time. What was I to do? I tagged along to school with my cousin, and the teacher, hearing my pitiful story, let me spend the morning. I turned up at home for lunch, said nothing about it to Lizzie (our maid), and went back to school in the afternoon. Someone (I suppose my grandmother) looked into the situation finally, made appropriate petitions, and I was allowed to stay, provided I got a smallpox vaccination. I could already read, so I made no trouble for the teacher. Later my cousin and I skipped a grade, too, so school was easy and fairly enjoyable.

My life, until I went to college, was confined to the Midwest. In the summer we had a month's sojourn on a lake. Many summers were spent at Palisades Park, on Lake Michigan. The Palisades were sand dunes and the beach wonderful. One memorable Thanksgiving, my Grandfather Jack took me with him to Decatur for the holiday. We stayed at my Aunt Jane's large house, where I had three cousins near my age, Jack, Anson, and Nancy. The whole clan (many Jacks lived in Decatur) had Thanksgiving dinner at my Great-Aunt Libbie's (my grandfather's sister Elizabeth). After dinner the company, old and young, danced Virginia Reels. It was wonderful except that a cousin my age (Cecile Jack) wore silver slippers, and mine were black patent leather Mary Janes. I was desperately envious. Later on, in high school years, I was on several occasions a guest at my Aunt Emily's in Kenilworth, Illinois. Kenilworth was a stylish suburb north of Chicago and Aunt Emily believed in style. I think she felt that she was giving me a taste of life as it ought to be lived.

My cousin Cassie and I attended the Peoria High School, which was actually pretty good. There was another one, below the bluff, known as the Manual Training High School. Needless to say, the school on the bluff got the best teachers and aimed higher for its students. Since I wanted to go to Smith, my mother's college, I had to prepare for the college board examinations. That meant 4 years of Latin and math, and a lot of extra preparation the last 2 years. Two other students, my friends Elizabeth Furst and Bill Miles, were also preparing for the boards, so we spent many afternoons and Saturdays together, with some very devoted teachers who tutored us. All three of us made it easily, Elizabeth to Smith with me, and Bill to Princeton, his father's school. My life in the Midwest essentially ended then.

Both my husband-to-be and I looked to the East, once he began his studies at Princeton and I mine at Smith, so the Midwest dimmed in our memories and plans. But it had served us well. Now two of our grandchildren have gone back to school there, Michael Gibson to Carleton College in Minnesota and Elizabeth Rosenberg to Oberlin in Ohio.

2

Becoming Psychologists

In 1922 James Gibson went off to Princeton to begin his sophomore year without much thought of what he was preparing for. Sophomore year at Princeton is the time when the clubs hold "bicker," a traditional name for looking over the underclassmen and inviting them (or not) to join clubs. Because James was a transfer student, he was unknown to the old boys of the clubs, and thus did not become a club member, a social disaster some might have thought, as from junior year on the students had meals at their clubs. However, James found a group of students to dine with, and better yet, found a group of students who were interested in the theater. Aside from debating, acting had been his only outside interest in high school, and he was enormously attracted to it. I never heard him mention the Triangle Club at Princeton (an acting group which was popular and pretty "clubby") but he became acquainted with a more serious organization, the Theatre Intime and mightily enjoyed his opportunities to act. The highlight of his stage career came his senior year. Since he cannot share the writing of this memoir with me, I quote from a short autobiography that he wrote for a psychological series (J.J. Gibson, 1967). Here he speaks for himself:

It was the Princeton celebrated by F. Scott Fitzgerald. I was an emancipated youth but, alas, not a gilded one. I was deeply impressed by that environment, like the unhappy novelist himself, but I dimly realized that I did not like it. However, in my last year we put on a production of a blood-and-thunder play of the twelfth century from the manuscript of which Shakespeare had stolen the plot of Hamlet. The characters were the same even if their speeches were bombast. It was a great success, especially the dueling, which I had coached, and we took it to New York for two nights. I fell in love with our Ophelia who had been borrowed from the cast of the Garrick Gaieties. This last was the first "intimate revue" produced in New York, and I became a familiar backstage visitor. Philosophy was neglected. I scraped through the comprehensive exams in May, however, and she came to my commencement in 1925. To be sure, she jilted me during the following year, when I was a graduate student, but I had become a sophisticate. I could stroll casually through a stage door. (p. 128)

Fig. 2. James Gibson,
a senior at Princeton.

Actually, James had another experience during his senior year that not only gave him great pleasure but determined the whole path of his life to follow. He had majored in philosophy and enjoyed his courses. He collected a great many philosophical works and continued to add to this library throughout his life, as well as making friends with philosophers at the institutions where he taught or visited. Philosophy may be a subject without content of its own, as my philosopher friend Marjorie Grene has often told me, but it appears to encourage deep and independent thinking. I believe that background played a role later in my husband's thoughtful and very tradition-breaking ideas about perception. Nonetheless, he encountered a new field that attracted him and determined his future. Again, I'll let him tell about it.

> At the beginning of my senior year I had taken a course in experimental psychology run in permissive fashion by H. S. Langfeld, newly arrived from Harvard. The eight students were a mixed group but an esprit de corps developed. Some catalyst was present that precipitated four psychologists from them: Bray, Gahagan, Gibson, and Schlosberg. Langfeld was delighted with us; he had a touch of the German professor, but he winked at the horseplay with which we enriched the laboratory exercises. Toward the end of the year he was able to offer three of us assistantships. This stroke of luck gave me an identity; I was an academic; not a philosopher, but even better, a psychologist. (J. J. Gibson, 1967, p. 128)

The following fall, he returned to Princeton as a graduate student and teaching assistant, along with Charles Bray and Harold Schlosberg, both of whom remained his lifelong friends. Members of the Psychology Department at Princeton included Langfeld, Howard Crosby Warren (a rather solemn but serious behaviorist), Leonard Carmichael, and E. B. Holt, a radical behaviorist, not solemn at all. I let my husband describe him:

> Holt was a slow writer but a great teacher. He had a contempt for humbug and a clarity of thought that has never been matched. He had shown how cognition might itself be a form of response, and he was engaged in extending conditioned reflex theory to social behavior, amending the gaps in the published textbook that his student Floyd Allport had recently written. He shocked his students by violent predictions in the mildest possible manner of speaking.
>
> Holt's motor theory of consciousness provided a way of encompassing the facts of Titchener without either trying to refute them or simply to forget about them. It was a more elegant theory than that of any other behaviorist. For thirty years I was reluctant to abandon it, and it is still very much alive to-

day, but the experimental evidence is now clearly against it. Awareness seems to me now an activity but not a motor activity, a form of adjustment that enhances the pickup of information but not a kind of behavior that alters the world. Instead of the contrast between consciousness and behavior that used to preoccupy us, I think we should look for the difference between observational activity and performatory activity. But this is getting ahead of the story. (J. J. Gibson, 1967, p. 129)

Holt presented him with copies of his books, inscribed to "Gibby." I still have them, part of a prized collection.

Graduate students at Princeton lived in the Graduate School. In fact, they dined there, wearing gowns, with a master sitting at a high table. Imitation of Oxford stopped there, however. The three psychology assistants attended seminars, graded undergraduates' papers, and wrote papers of their own. Life was not hard. Bray and Schlosberg told me a story about my husband that I include principally for my grandchildren. James loved to sleep late and apparently often did. One day, Bray and Schlosberg returned to the graduate school for lunch, bearing a message for James from Langfeld, his mentor, who wished to see him at once. They got James out of bed, and left him, in his pajamas, one foot on a chair, opening a newly arrived issue of *The New Yorker*. They returned from lunch a half hour later and found him still with one foot on the chair, finishing *The New Yorker*.

James got on with his mentor, nonetheless, and Langfeld was his thesis director. His research was on form perception and drawing forms from memory. He had loved geometry in high school, so this was perhaps a natural choice. Again, I let him speak:

I did my thesis on the drawing of visual forms from memory to refute the just-published results of Wulf at Berlin, a student of Koffka's, purporting to show that memories changed spontaneously toward better *Gestalten*. The drawing of *my* subjects differed from the originals only in accordance with laws of perceptual habit, not laws of dynamic self-distribution, I concluded with great confidence. Form perception was learned. Otherwise one fell into the arms of Immanuel Kant. I was a radical empiricist, like Holt, who suspected that the very structure of the nervous system itself was learned by neurobiotaxis in accordance with the laws of conditioning. Little did I know that within six months I would be facing Koffka himself weekly across a seminar table. (J. J. Gibson, 1967, pp. 129–130)

The three young assistants duly finished their PhD's in June of 1928, and good jobs were found for all (times seem to have been good for psychology then). Bray stayed at Princeton, Schlosberg went to Brown, and Gibson went to Smith College, going their own ways but to meet often in the future.

At Smith, as he intimated, James met Kurt Koffka, who had been brought there by William Allen Neilson, Smith's president, without consulting his Psychology Department. Koffka was given his own place to work (an old house), not on campus or near the college's psychology building. That was just as well, as he installed a number of followers, including a group we dubbed the "Mad Russians", all psychologists from Europe. The Smith Psychology Department included, among others, William Sentman Taylor (chairman), who taught abnormal psychology; Margaret Curti, who taught animal and child psychology; and Harold Israel (an old student of Boring), who taught history and systems. James taught perception and experimental psychology. There was, actually, a fairly large group of psychologists altogether, and it promoted a lively community with good discussions. The experimental psychology class was a whole-year course, for majors with a good background. I'll leave it now, but come back to it later.

James had a great bachelor's life at Smith, making friends such as Newton Arvin, who taught American literature, and Sydney Deane, a classicist, with whom he dined (with others) at a super boarding house run by Miss Sherman, a very proper Southern lady. He became close friends with Oliver Larkin of the Art Department, who directed amateur plays on the side, so that the theater became available again. He lost no time in getting involved in Larkin's amateur productions, made many friends (both faculty and townspeople), and enjoyed it all thoroughly. No students took part in Larkin's plays, but James did not neglect his students, especially in his experimental class. Neither did he neglect his profession. He soon published his thesis and set out on a new research program of his own creation, research on adaptation to figural aspects of forms, such as curvature, which was to make him a reputation. As early as 1933, he published a major paper on this new topic, "Adaptation, After-effect, and Contrast in the Perception of Curved Lines" (J. J. Gibson, 1933). The project had its birth in his advanced experimental class, which I let him describe:

> My specialty was advanced experimental psychology, which met six hours a week for thirty-two weeks a year. There were always eight to a dozen seniors in it, and we ran experiments on every possible problem. They were generally new experiments, with little or no published evidence as to what the results might be. Bright students, especially girls, will work like demons when the outcome will be a contribution to knowledge. At the high point of the course the students would choose a problem from my offerings, run the subjects, analyze

the data, and write up a report at the rate of one a month. I still have copies of the best of these papers, and every so often I find a published experiment that was first performed essentially by one of my students in the thirties. A good many were publishable. The apparatus was makeshift (but it was used only once), the statistics were elementary (but one gets a feeling for reliability), and a satisfying number of the questions we put to test gave clear answers. There must have been 500 or more such projects in my years at Smith, and I am sure that they constitute my main backlog of psychological knowledge. And there is still another backlog in the files of unanswered questions that I had to dream up in order to keep ahead of those lovely creatures who had a zeal for discovering how the mind works. (J. J. Gibson, 1967, p. 131)

James stayed on at Smith, despite at least one good offer (from Dartmouth, I believe), and that was indeed my good fortune, as I now tell.

I took the college boards at the age of 16 in June 1927, and in midsummer was waiting to hear the results at the summer home of Bill Miles's parents in northern Michigan. Bill had heard a week earlier that he was accepted at Princeton, when I, by that time very anxious, found a telegram hidden in my napkin at lunchtime. The news was good, but the telegram had been withheld since early morning and I ceased to regard my hostess, Bill's mother, as a potential mother-in-law. (Bill, however, remained a potential date at Princeton.) Elizabeth Furst, our friend and fellow student, was also accepted at Smith and eager preparations were made.

Elizabeth and I set off for Northampton, Massachusetts, accompanied by her mother. Neither of us had ever been east of Illinois, so it was an adventure and a bit daunting. We were both assigned to Hopkins House B, one of the older houses on campus with the advantage of looking out on Paradise Pond, just across a campus road from us. Paradise is a beautiful small lake, named by Jenny Lind when she was on a concert tour in Northampton (or so tradition had it). Elizabeth and I decided not to room together, in order to promote new friendships. My roommate was Clara Farr Taft, Boston bred, educated in an exclusive prep school, and 3 years older than I. She had a nickname, Bunny, and she immediately dubbed me Jackie. We got on very well, despite the difference in our backgrounds, and I found I was quite able to do the work and enjoyed my courses. Our first holiday was Thanksgiving, with only 1 day free. My roommate's paternal grandmother sent her chauffeur (called James, of course) in a "town-car" to drive Bunny to her home in Arlington, an exclusive Boston suburb, for Thanksgiving dinner. I was invited to go along. Her grandmother inspected me through a lorgnette and said, "Where did you say you come from?" The only other diners were Bunny's rather elderly aunt and uncle who lived with her grandmother. Bunny's parents were divorced. After dinner, James drove us back to Northampton. I never repeated that visit, but I often visited at Bunny's mother's apartment in Boston, not formidable at all.

College was everything I had hoped, and I loved Smith. One of my courses was Psychology 101, a whole-year course with labs. I continued with psychology my sophomore year, taking animal psychology first term (again with lab, but a rat lab this time) and child psychology second term. I'm afraid I was rather remiss about outside activities at college. It was more fun to spend weekends away at men's colleges. I went frequently to Princeton and I went to Dartmouth carnival. My first visit to Princeton with Bill Miles was in the fall of my freshman year. My mother thought I ought to be well chaperoned, so she arranged for me to stay with a second cousin of hers, Beth Scoon. Beth was a daughter of John Grier Hibben, then president of Princeton, and she had married a Professor Scoon, a philosopher. They were very pleasant and hospitable, but on Sunday they expected Bill and me to go to the University chapel service and afterward to lunch at the president's house. Lunch was very formal, with butlers and ambassadorial guests, making Bill and me feel like the freshmen we were. I stayed with the Scoons other times, but never had to repeat the Sunday lunch.

I decided, when the time came, to major in psychology, although I had earlier supposed that I would major in languages. However, my family couldn't afford to send me abroad to study for my junior year, as most language majors did, because the Great Depression had arrived. It was hard enough just to pay the college bills! But I was interested in psychology and had gained more respect for and interest in science as my intellectual horizon expanded. My junior year was a happy and successful one, ending with an invitation to stay on for commencement and serve as a "junior usher." That invitation included helping to carry the ivy chain in the seniors' procession. I was attired in a blue organdy dress, made by my mother. I wore it again on Sunday afternoon, when I was detailed to serve punch to the seniors' parents at the official garden party. Unfortunately, it rained, and I hovered in a covered corner next to my assigned station. Also hovering there was Assistant Professor James J. Gibson. He had been posted there to shake hands officially with parents of his graduating seniors. It was a day to mark on the family calendar.

James Gibson and I not only met that day; he drove me back to my dormitory in his ancient Model T Ford (not improving the blue organdy gown). The next morning, before catching my train home, I rushed to the dean's office and changed my fall schedule to include Professor James Gibson's course in advanced experimental psychology.

The class in experimental psychology was truly a turning point in my life. There were 8 or 10 students in the class (Priscilla Cahill, Sylvia Hazelton, Gertrude Raffel, Mimi Ramer, and Hilda Richardson are the names I remember, all bright and hard working). Sylvia and I did an experiment that involved wearing wedge prisms and measuring auditory localization as it gradually shifted along with adaptation to the prisms. Gertrude and I did an experiment on transfer of a conditioned finger withdrawal that actually got published in the *Journal of Experimental Psychology*. All the experiments were new and exciting and as the year wore on, I discovered what my chosen métier was to be. I wanted to be a real psychologist and do experiments. I went to see the chairman of the Psychology Department, Professor Taylor, and asked if the department might have such a bonanza as a teaching assistantship available for the following year. Fortune smiled on me. It did, and I was appointed to one.

As it happened, three teaching assistantships were available, and they went to Hulda Rees (another senior), Sylvia Hazelton, and me. We were paid $800 for the year and were expected to work half-time and embark on graduate study toward an MA the other half. Hulda and I found an attic

Fig. 3. Eleanor Jack
on graduation day

apartment to share ($40 per month). I graduated magna cum laude, but my parents couldn't attend commencement—too expensive to come east. My mother's cousin, Jean Morron, had returned for her reunion, however, and represented my family. Everyone was pleased at my good fortune, and I could hardly wait for the fall term to begin.

So, in September of 1931 the three new assistants began their teaching and graduate careers. Each of us taught two lab sections in the same introductory course that I had taken my freshman year. There were 30 students in each section, which meant grading 60 lab reports per week, as well as preparing ourselves to teach the labs and setting them up. I never learned faster in my life. It was thrilling and a challenge and we adored every moment of it. We attended some graduate seminars too, with only a small enrollment, and learned what it was like to present a report and be put on the spot. Learning to do research was the major concern, and at the beginning of the second year we each chose a topic for work on a master's thesis.

One needed a supervisor for a master's thesis and I chose (not surprisingly) Professor Gibson. I wanted to work on memory, a fashionable topic at the time. I decided, after immersing myself in the relevant literature, that I wanted to work on retroactive inhibition (a concept assumed to explain forgetting) and that I wanted to challenge the current vogue for analyzing tasks into shared identical elements to explain transfer or interference. James Gibson, my advisor, favored a functional view, and we decided to describe the tasks I was going to use in terms of "operation" and "material," for comparison in a transfer-like setup. My thesis experiment varied both operation and material (separately and together) in a typical retroactive inhibition paradigm. Operation turned out to be just as important as material, a victory for the functionalists.

Meanwhile, the advisor and advisee were becoming well acquainted, and before the thesis was completed, we were thoroughly in love. The thesis was accepted and published in the *American Journal of Psychology*, and I was appointed Instructor for the following year, having won my MA. The MA did not make me a real psychologist, but it was a big step on the way. I could not afford to go away to graduate school yet (the Great Depression was at its height), so the instructorship was perfect, especially because James Gibson and I were now married.

We were married in the summer of 1932, in Peoria, Illinois, at my parents' home. Only family and relatives and a few of my local friends were invited, but the relatives made quite a show. There were my great-aunts from Decatur and my Grandfather Jack, of course; James's parents and my mother-in-law's sister and her family came from Ohio. The wedding was in

September, so we hurried back to Northampton to get settled and begin classes. Hulda moved out of the attic apartment and James moved in with me. The landlady reduced the rent to $33 a month.

As an instructor, I taught labs again, and now also discussion sections, still in the introductory course; and I assisted in the animal psychology course, which I really liked. But I still needed a PhD. After 2 years of this life, I applied to the Yale graduate school. I was admitted (that was a concession for a woman), but I was offered no scholarship or assistance of any kind. Smith, my generous and wonderful alma mater, awarded me the Harriet Boyd Hawes scholarship of $325, which I could take elsewhere. The $325 paid my tuition at Yale, which was $300 per annum, and left me $25, besides.

I want to digress here to sing the praises of Smith College, the greatest possible contrast to Yale (at that time) as regards women's education. Smith, a women's college, was a place where women were not only permitted to be scholars, but encouraged, even in the sciences. Perhaps that is true now of the big men's universities that have opened their doors to women, but I

Fig. 4. Eleanor and James Gibson at their wedding.

doubt that the atmosphere for encouraging a woman who wants to be a scholar even now matches the atmosphere of a women's college.

I went to Yale alone, but my husband had his first sabbatical coming, and could join me second semester. We managed quite a few weekends together, too. Meanwhile, I had to conquer a system of graduate education intended for men only. There were a few other women graduate students in psychology, but they were a small fraction of the 40 or 50 total. Again, I had to find an advisor. Because I was attracted to animal psychology, I approached Professor Robert L. Yerkes, who had a chimpanzee laboratory right there in New Haven. I had to wait 10 days or more to see him, but was finally admitted by his secretary to his presence. He did not invite me to sit down, but inquired, "What can I do for you?" I answered that I had come to request that he be my advisor. He rose, walked to the door and held it open, saying, "I have no women in my laboratory."

I believe now that it was expected, when I was admitted, that I would either work with Professor Arnold Gesell, a child psychologist who did have women (all kowtowing to him) in his laboratory, or else in a kind of University testing operation run by Dr. Catherine Miles, wife of Professor Walter Miles (he referred to her, always, as "Dr. Catherine"). The other two women students had chosen one or the other of these options, but I was determined not to. I wanted "hard science" and an opportunity to do experiments.

All first-year graduate students in the Yale Psychology Department had to take a so-called proseminar, no matter what their previous experience. There were 10 students enrolled in my year, from very different backgrounds. All the major professors in the department had a couple of weeks' session with this group, and it continued all year. We read through a bibliography chosen by each professor, gave reports to the group, and were given a written examination at the end of each session. The chairman, Professor Roswell P. Angier, opened the first session with readings on the history of psychology, using very ancient and yellowed notes. He was a kindly man, however, and informed us that we would be ranked from 1 to 10 on each of our examinations, and that, at the end of the year, the two students with lowest rankings would be dropped. (They were.)

My colleagues in this seminar included Irvin Child, Austin Riesen, and Vincent Nowlis, all to become prominent psychologists. I was not worried about the competition however, and made many good friends. Dick and Adella Youtz, second-year graduate students, became two of my best friends. They had a sort of dinner club in their small apartment. The participants included Austin Riesen, Mac McGarvey (a third-year graduate student), and myself. It was indeed my good fortune to be included. We talked about everything at dinner, and afterward walked the long, cold mile and a half through the slums to the Medical School Library, where we pored over reading assignments until closing time. It was a very cold walk back, through a dubious neighborhood, so it was a good thing to have company.

My companions suggested after many discussions that I should consider Professor Clark Hull for my advisor (if he would have me). Clark Hull was one of the big guns of the time, interested in learning theory and transfer, working on a system with axioms and proofs much like geometry. His axioms (or principles as I would have preferred to call them) were all taken from the conditioned reflex literature and included concepts like inhibition of various kinds and irradiation. Experiments were run, for the most part on rats, to test the predictions that fell out of the system. After long thought, I believed that I might be able to apply some of the concepts (generalization and differential inhibition) to human verbal learning and memory. I was, in fact, attracted by the logic and experimental checking of the enterprise. It seemed like hard-headed science and that appealed to me.

I made an appointment with Professor Hull and at least was not ushered out. (He was lame and walked with difficulty, leaning on a cane.) I explained that I needed an advisor for my dissertation. He then explained to me that he only accepted students who were willing to work with his methods and use his concepts. I told him about my interest in verbal learning and memory and said I thought I might be able to put together a system predicting transfer and forgetting using the concepts of generalization and differential inhibition. He did not look convinced but told me that he would need to see my ideas written out in some detail. So much for that, for the moment.

I had only 1 year to spend in New Haven, during which I had to pass a number of examinations. In addition to the prosem exams, there were a statistics exam, two foreign language exams, and a major field examination. I accomplished the first three with no trouble, doing well in the proseminar (my 2 years of graduate study at Smith had taught me a lot). But I could not take a major field examination until I had a field, and that meant an advisor. It would be his field, of course. I managed to write out my ideas for Hull before the year finished, and I was accepted. He gave me quantities of material to read. I could come back sometime late next year and take the field examination that he would prepare for me. The dissertation research I would perform later at Smith, which was, happily, taking me back as an instructor.

My husband spent the second term in New Haven with me, writing, getting a little research done, and teaching a small class (one member of it was Robert Gagné, who I return to later). We found a furnished apartment on the second floor of a store building at a major intersection. Streetcars ran down one street and a truck route down the other. Whoever lived above us had noisy brawls, with thumps like falling bodies occurring occasionally. However, we spent most of our time at the Institute of Human Relations, as the large, newish building psychology shared with anthropology and sociology was called. It was built in the slum area near the medical school, not on the Yale campus. Presumably, research on human relations was at home there.

One memorable social incident during my year in New Haven stands out. On my 25th birthday in December, my new Yale friends had a party for me. It was held at an old, small auditorium with a balcony, a building then housing some kind of University testing service. Mac McGarvey had a part-time job there, so he could commandeer the site for the party, which was held on the balcony (all the desks and files were downstairs). My husband came from Northampton, of course, and brought with him my good friend and ex-roommate Hulda Rees. It was clear before the evening was over that Mac and Hulda had fallen hard for one another. A year or so later they were married. When Mac finished his PhD, he found a job at Mt. Holyoke College, ideally (for us) near Northampton. Tragically, he died only 2 years later.

When we returned to Northampton, we did not move back to the attic, but into a new real ground-floor apartment on High Street. It was away from the center of town in an attractive spot, across the street from the DeGogorzas. Maitland DeGogorza was a faculty member, a friend, and had just married Julia, one of his talented seniors in the Art Department. The neighborhood was pleasant, and we had a tiny spare room for a guest, but I needed to work furiously for my field exam and then to plan my dissertation, which eventually consisted of a long formal theoretical introduction and four major experiments. I finally finished it all and was awarded my PhD in June of 1938. Now I was a real psychologist. The Smith College faculty rewarded me by appointing me Assistant Professor, and I prepared my dissertation for publication, proudly getting four journal articles out of it, a theoretical one published in the *Psychological Review* and the other three in the *Journal of Experimental Psychology*.

3

Teaching and Life at Smith College

Smith College not only kept me on while I finished my dissertation; I was now an assistant professor. My husband had already achieved tenure and was an associate professor. He was publishing and becoming well known in the field of perception because of his work on adaptation to geometrical features of forms such as curvature and inclination. These were relational attributes, and a new theory of perception (not sensation-based) was called for. I let James Gibson tell about his surprising discovery:

> I did an experiment that summer (1932) before getting married. I had previously been using a pair of spectacle frames with optometrist's trial-prisms in them to verify the old result that one soon learned to reach for things in the right direction despite their apparent displacement. I had also observed the curvature adaptation that resulted from wearing the prisms and assumed that this too was a correction of visual experience in accordance with Bishop Berkeley's theory of visual perception. But there was disturbing evidence against this presumably self-evident explanation (even in Stratton's original

experiment of this type), and I thought of a control experiment that would surely put the doctrine of sensory empiricism back on its feet. I would look at a field of *actually* curved lines equivalent to the prismatic distortion for as long as I could stand to do so and show that no change in apparent curvature would then occur. But to my astonishment it did occur. Apparent curvature still decreased and straight lines thereafter looked curved in the opposite direction. (J. J. Gibson 1967, pp. 132–133)

This research was his first step toward the conviction that optical transformations over time are the real "carriers of information, not optical forms frozen in time" (J. J. Gibson, 1967, pp. 132–133). It was a discovery full of implications, leading to a broad research program and enhancing his reputation as an experimentalist. The course in experimental psychology continued to prosper, providing material for James to edit a monograph (J. J. Gibson, 1935), titled *Studies in Psychology from Smith College*, all papers authored by his students with him.

His interests were broader than his professional life, however. His interest in the theater had never lapsed, and our good friend Oliver Larkin, a professor in the Art Department, a gifted director, put on plays for the Northampton Players, an amateur town and gown theater group. He frequently gave James a part. I remember one play, called *Good-Bye Again*, a kind of satirization of Hollywood. James had a lead part, and I was given a couple of "walk-on" parts. One of them had a line to speak, "The Elks are in Bermuda." I practiced it over and over with every conceivable inflection. I was awkward and uncomfortable with the whole thing, and decided henceforth to be a makeup expert. I did this (with no training) to the satisfaction of the players, so I still got in on the fun.

The other nonacademic interest that drew my husband and many fellow faculty members at the time was the political scene. We were in the very depths of the Great Depression and there was serious social unrest. Like many academics, we tended toward the left. My husband was drawn into a group that was soon dubbed "radical." Professor Larkin and economics professor Dorothy Douglas were in fact said to be communists. I never knew whether they really were or not, but we went along with the major action, which was to form a teachers' union. The idea was to show our sympathy and identification with organized labor. Smith's President, William Allen Neilson, was a far-sighted and liberal man. He chastised no one for their politics, but the label of "radical" was applied by some members of the community, inevitably, and stuck for many years, even being recalled and publicized years later when communists were attacked in the McCarthy era.

James's liberal tendencies had one real and valuable outcome. He had never studied or felt attracted to social psychology, but a national organization was formed for "The Psychological Study of Social Issues", and he was persuaded by friends more active in social psychology to join. At about the same time, Professor Rogers, the oldest member of Smith's Psychology Department, retired. He had always taught the course in social psychology. It was not very popular (actually boring, students said), but of course it had to be taught. After much departmental discussion of alternatives, James (with strong misgivings) agreed to take it on. He was totally unprepared as regarded the standard textbook literature in the field, but he was persuaded of the topic's potential relevance to the social and economic problems of the times. It was during the "New Deal" days, and everything was astir. James struggled mightily to keep his new course on a proper scientific basis, but he was also determined to relate it to the serious concerns of the times. The enrollment in the course rapidly shot up, and students devoted to social problems haunted the halls. Things were clearly on the right track. The whole field was beginning to change. Despite his growing interest, James never became active in research in social psychology. His heart was firmly in his experimental course, where the experiments were almost always "cognitive", as we say now, on perception, learning, and remembering.

His interests even in perception were geared to reality, however. He and a local friend, Pete Crooks, an engineer, wrote a remarkable paper on automobile driving. I let James speak again:

> In 1937, one of my friends, an engineer, was a bug on automobiles, and it was the time of the first driver clinics. The tests being given, I felt, were nonsense, for the skill of driving a car (on which I prided myself) had never been analyzed. So we analyzed it (with L. E. Crooks, 1938). Lewin had begun to formulate his theory of behavior as locomotion, with fields, valences, and vectors, but it was static and did not apply very well to visually-guided real locomotion, so other concepts had to be worked out—the clearance-lines of obstacles, the margin of safety considered as a ratio, and the temporal flow of the necessary information for accelerating, decelerating, and steering. Our paper was not spectacular, but the problems came up again in my wartime work on aircraft landing (1947, 1955) and my later attempt at a general theory of locomotion (1958). No fact of behavior, it seems to me, betrays the weakness of the old concept of visual stimuli so much as the achieving of contact without collision—for example, the fact that a bee can land on a flower without blundering into it. The reason can only be that centrifugal flow of the structure of the bee's optic array specifies locomotion and controls the flow of locomotor responses. (J. J. Gibson, 1967, p. 134)

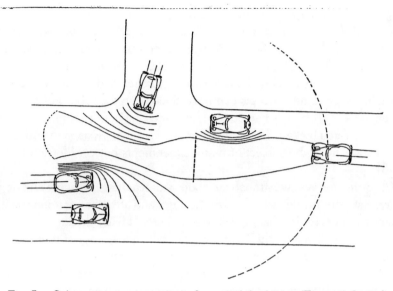

Fig. 5.   Schematic representation of automobile driving (Figure 1 from J.
J. Gibson and L. Crooks, 1938, "A Theorectical Field-Analysis of
Automobile-Driving," The American Journal of Psychology, 51, 453–471.

This paper might have been sent for publication to *The Journal of Applied Psychology* or even to an engineering journal. But James Gibson (perhaps with tongue in cheek) thought to beard the lion in his den. He sent the paper to *The American Journal of Psychology*, the country's oldest and most respected journal, founded by Titchener, and at that time edited by Boring, Titchener's student and faithful follower. Boring was the author of a well-known history of psychology, which we had all had to plow through, and of a volume entitled *The Physical Dimensions of Consciousness* (Boring, 1933), in which he argued that sensations, linked to physical stimuli, were the stuff of consciousness and thus constituted the entire subject matter of psychology. Somewhat to our surprise, he accepted the paper at once, accompanied by a letter (he was a great letter writer) saying, "I love your paper about how Lewin drives a car!" A conservative, rather scholastic psychologist himself, Boring was generous to younger psychologists and gave full attention to their more liberal views. The paper's illustrations (drawings of little cars with "clearance-lines" around them, obstacles approaching, etc.) greatly added to the attractiveness of the journal. I include here the first figure from the paper, showing a driver viewing a traffic situation in which he or she must quickly perceive the "minimum stopping zone." This paper was, as I now recognize, a forerunner of many later theoretical research papers, for example a general paper on locomotion written many years later at Oxford University, recently reprinted in *The Journal of Ecological Psychology*. The early paper did not describe the stimulus information, as later papers did, but the functional approach and the dynamics were there. So were some concepts that have since been the subject of much research: One was obstacle perception and perceiving "time to contact" (mathematically treated by Lee, 1976); another, the idea that perception and action are "prospective," the subject of many experiments by von Hofsten (1980, 1993).

My own time was very much taken up with teaching, planning and doing the research for my dissertation, writing it up, and after that rewriting it all in separate papers for journal publication. I felt that I had humanized the concepts of generalization and differentiation, taking them out of their original context of the conditioned reflex and using them as functional concepts for understanding problems of human learning. I must give Hull credit here (which he is seldom given) for wanting to do this very thing, however austere his "logico-deductive" method of theorizing. I was greatly influenced, for example, by his paper called "A Functional Interpretation of the Conditioned Reflex" (Hull, 1929). His papers on the goal gradient (Hull, 1932) and the habit–family hierarchy (Hull, 1934) were further attempts to do this. The "habit–family" paper was an attempt to give a theoretical explanation for the flexibility of everyday behavior, seeking to overcome the obvious inflexibility of the conditioned reflex. The problem is still with us.

Our local group of collegial psychologists had been increased, as I mentioned earlier, by President Neilson's appointment of Kurt Koffka to a kind of special professorship at Smith. Koffka held a regular weekly seminar for graduate students and any colleagues who cared to attend, and a fair number of us pretty regularly did. It offered an opportunity for discussion and reports of timely research. Neither my husband nor I was particularly attracted by Gestalt psychology. My husband was too busy seeking a satisfactory theory of perception of his own, and I was much more attracted by "hard-headed" science, but we made friends in the group, among them Grace and Fritz Heider. Fritz had come to this country, I believe under Koffka's aegis, and taken a research position at the Clarke School for the Deaf, which was situated in Northampton. Grace was already a psychologist at the school, and they were soon mutually attracted and married. We gradually came to know them well, and they remained lifelong friends. They had three sons, one of them now a professor of anthropology at the University of South Carolina. He is an intimate friend of my son, and now the Heiders's and Gibsons's grand-children are friends.

Because our academic community was not as large as those at the major universities, we were particularly concerned to make and keep friends among psychologists elsewhere, and to attend gatherings of the Eastern and the American Psychological Associations. Of course, we aimed to (and usually did) give papers at them, too. They were fun, because one reuned with old graduate school friends, made new friends, and came home with fresh ideas. The national scene in psychology at the time was dominated by a self-important, austere, senior group of 40 to 50 psychologists, all full professors with reputations, known as the Society of Experimental Psychologists. Members were elected by secret ballot, only a couple of new ones each year as the seniors died off. Edwin G. Boring, of Harvard, was the acknowledged "head" of this group.[1] He was the heir of Edward Bradford Titchener, founder of the Society. Boring took his PhD at Cornell with Titchener in 1914. He was married, strange as it may seem, to another psychologist, Lucy May Boring. She also completed a PhD with Titchener in 1912 (even stranger!). But as her obituary observed, her career as a psychologist was very short, although she lived to be 110 years old. Lucy Boring taught for 1 year at Vassar College and 1 year at Wells, both women's colleges "before giving up a career for family life" (her words; see Furumoto, 1998). But, as she later said, she "read (and advised) every book and article my husband wrote." Lucy Boring was undoubtedly a gifted woman (very few women obtained PhDs in 1912). She was never invited to join a meeting of the Experimentalists, however.

No young men were either, even in 1936. A small group of young Eastern psychologists (all men) decided that it was time to form a new exclusive group. The first rule was that retirement would take place, automatically, when the member reached the age of 40. It was run by an "autocratic minority", originally composed of C. H. Graham (Brown University), W. A. Hunt (Connecticut College for Women), C. Jacobsen and D. Marquis (Yale), E. B. Newman (Swarthmore College), and S. S. Stevens (Harvard). Other young psychologists invited to join included James Gibson. The group called itself the Psychological Round Table (PRT; see Benjamin, 1977). Meetings were held annually the first weekend in December. It was expected that each member would speak about his research and that all would have a good time. They did. A favorite place for meeting was the Wiggins Tavern in Northampton. I occasionally helped make the arrangements, but I was never invited to attend a meeting. Actually, James Gibson was elected a member of the Society of Experimental Psychologists in 1939, when he was 35 years old, but (no surprise) he found the PRT more enjoyable.

---

[1] I owned and gave to the Cornell Library Archives a transcript of Boring's address to the group on its 50th anniversary. See Boring (1938, 1967).

Meanwhile, full-time teaching, which now included the course in animal psychology, plus rewriting my dissertation for publication (E. Gibson, 1939, 1940, 1941, 1942), and a master's student whose thesis I supervised, kept me busy. I was also by degrees learning to cook. (I had never learned at home because we had a cook who didn't like children in her kitchen.) Our apartment on High Street had a real kitchen, so a little domesticity was in order. Meanwhile, the Great Depression hit its very lowest ebb. We were approached, I suppose as a promising young couple, by an agent trying to sell us a house. The house was owned by a young, recently widowed lady who wished to move away and marry again. It was an old house (built about 1800), white clapboard, with five fireplaces, and lilacs around the door. It was on Elm Street, a couple of blocks beyond the college. We warded off the agent, but he came again and again, each time lowering the price. He finally said the owner was so eager to sell that the price was down to $5,000. That was hard to resist for a beautiful old house, but our savings were as yet pretty lean. How could we do it? That Christmas my Grandfather Jack gave each of his grandchildren a gift of $1,000. Done! With our savings, it was nearly enough for a down- payment. James's father and a friend gave us loans and we bought the house!

It needed some remodeling inside, in particular removal of a wall that divided the central downstairs area into two rooms, one very small and useless. With the wall down, and the help of an architect who taught at the college and knew everything about old New England houses, we gained a wonderful living room. It was the original kitchen and had a mammoth fireplace, with two side warming cupboards and a powder cupboard above it. The front room (with another fireplace) became the study. There were fireplaces upstairs as well (never used by us). It was a wonderful house.

We were particularly lucky to have acquired the house, because it soon appeared that we were going to need more room. We had decided, when we married, that children should be postponed until I had won my PhD But now I had it, I was an assistant professor, my husband had tenure, and we felt that precautions could be relaxed. I became pregnant in 1939, not long after we bought the house. The baby was due in early February 1940. I decided to ask for a leave for the second term of that year. Unlike Lucy Boring, I had no thought of giving up my career as a psychologist, but I could hold it up a little for a baby. I went to William Allen Neilson, Smith's president, and explained my request. He answered, with a twinkle, that he recommended settling it with my chairman. My husband, as it happened, was chairman that year (a job he did not welcome, but the chairman was on leave). So I was given a semester's leave, and kept my job on the faculty. I think only a forward-looking women's college would have done that in 1939.

Fig. 6. Eleanor and James Gibson in front of the fireplace
at 210 Elm Street.

The baby came (James J. Gibson, Jr., to be called Jerry for his middle
name, Jerome), was healthy and throve, and the house was a joy. A little
room next to ours was just right for a baby. I got accustomed to caring for a
baby, doing laundry, making formula, and keeping up with the general daily
routine. But it seemed to take all my time. What were we going to do come
September, when I was due to teach full time again? We pondered the question as summer came and the delighted grandparents visited. Eventually we
hit on a solution that really worked.

We put advertisements in the local papers (usually weeklies) of small
towns and country villages in western Massachusetts. We said that a young
working couple with a baby needed a live-in housekeeper who had had experience with children. We asked for a written reply, because we wanted to
be sure of a literate person. One of our respondents sounded very promising,
a widow who had raised three now-grown children, at that time keeping
house for a lone widower in a small country town. We hired a babysitter and

went to see her. She was a gray-haired, pleasant-faced, pleasant-voiced woman. I asked why she wanted to leave her present position. She said she was bored and lonesome, and would like to live with young people and help care for a young child. My husband asked, "Can you make apple pie?" She said that was one of her specialties, and he was hooked. So, Mrs. Baldwin came to live with us. She loved Jerry, really could cook, and obviously knew what she was doing. We paid her $10 a week, and I hired someone else to do weekly cleaning. It was a success, partly I think because the house was large and we all enjoyed sufficient privacy. My classes went smoothly, my time with my young son was all enjoyable, and Mrs. Baldwin was happy to live in a larger town. She sang in a church choir, took Jerry for daily walks and showed him off to passers-by, and kept us well fed. She stayed with us until World War II came along and made drastic changes in everyone's lives.

4

World War II

On Sunday, December 7, 1941, I was playing with Jerry and contemplating the next day's lecture. James was away at a meeting of the PRT, a "raffish group of young psychologists", as my husband called it (J. J. Gibson, 1967, p. 133). The telephone rang and a friend's voice said, "Turn on your radio, if you haven't already." Excited voices on every station proclaimed the news of Japan's surprise attack on Pearl Harbor. What a way to celebrate my birthday! I was 31 years old that day. My husband was driving home from the meeting and had barely heard the news. When he returned, we pondered over what would happen next, but we didn't have long to wait to find out. Our country was at war with Japan, and very soon with the Axis powers as well. President Neilson had brought a number of European refugees to Smith, and we had become good friends with many of them. They had escaped with little or nothing except their education, so we were prepared to be sympathetic with America's attempts to change conditions in Europe.

Only a few months later, my husband was called on to help. The Army Air Force was setting up a program to prepare tests that would assist in the effective selection of air crew personnel—pilots, navigators, bombardiers, the whole lot. Landing a plane, evading enemy fighters, and firing at moving planes were all tasks that required excellent perceptual ability. There were no appropriate tests presently in existence. An expert on perception seemed to be just what was needed (even though the expert had no experience with testing or flying, only with laboratory experiments). The program was to be planned and its personnel put together and assigned jobs in Washington, DC, before moving off (presumably) to some field base. Captain James Gibson left for Washington, DC, not long into the second semester. His departure created a difficulty in handling the classes he would have been teaching. The biggest problem was social psychology. No one left in the department felt competent to teach it or had time for another big course. The problem was solved (we thought), when Professor Richard Sollenberger, who taught social psychology at Mt. Holyoke College, agreed to come to Northampton a couple of times a week and do double duty. That solution worked for a couple of months, but before the end of the term, Captain Sollenberger departed, too. It was fortunate for both colleges that our friends the Heiders were in Northampton and could take leaves from their present pursuits.

Fig. 7. Captain James Gibson with Jerry, spring, 1942.

Grace Heider (a Mt. Holyoke graduate) did some teaching at Mt. Holyoke, and Fritz Heider, to his real pleasure I believe (see Heider, 1995), took over some of James's responsibilities. He was a perception psychologist himself, so that part of his new responsibilities fit well.

Meanwhile, final examinations had to be given to the now very large social psychology class. Dick Sollenberger, with help from James on a weekend visit home, prepared an examination, but in the end I, with little self-assurance, graded the papers. It was a busy June. Life became even busier as decisions had to be made about our plans for the immediate future. I did not want to stay in Northampton being a wartime widow for the foreseeable future. Plans had been made to establish the psychological testing and research unit to which my husband was assigned under the aegis of the new Flying Training Command, for the time being at least, at the Command's headquarters. For some reason, the headquarters was to be set up in a large, new office building in Fort Worth, Texas. All the new officers were urged to bring their families along to Fort Worth, even with furniture (as the army would pay for the move). We eventually decided that Jerry and I should go along, because it looked more and more like a long war. We rented a house (unseen and unfurnished) in Fort Worth, and felt lucky to rent our beloved Northampton home to the wife of a physician who had been called up and expected to go overseas. She thought it best to move, too, and had friends in Northampton. We bade goodbye to Mrs. Baldwin, who had no trouble finding another place.

So, before midsummer we left Northampton (shipping ahead a minimum of furniture), and headed for the battle of Fort Worth, as we soon referred to it. I was going to be an Army wife, living in a state I had never visited, with my extremely academic husband in a uniform. Fort Worth in August, as to be expected, was incredibly hot. But I had made my choice. It was either stay at home, teach a heavy load, and be a single mother, or go with my husband (for as long as I could) and perhaps add to our family. I have never regretted the decision.

The families that came along to Fort Worth with the psychological section of the Flying Training Command became our good friends. They included the Geldards, the Hennemans, the Sollenbergers, the Ghisellis, the Kemps, the Carters, and other academics less well known to psychologists nowadays. The men formed a carpool to drive to work, and the wives made an occasional joint visit to a PX nearby. Gasoline was closely rationed, so no one had the luxury of shopping around alone. A bonus was a country club quite nearby offering free use of its facilities to the officers of the Flying Training Command. The club had a large swimming pool and tennis courts,

which we soon availed ourselves of. Wives and children spent the afternoons in the pool, trying to escape the fierce heat. Sunday mornings all the
new psychological officers gathered at the tennis courts. They were ordered
to exercise, and tennis matches offered a handy and social means. Wives
and children came along and cheered them on, making it a social occasion.

The work that went on among the new officers of the Aviation Psychology Program was not a matter of great satisfaction to them, however. Few of
them had any experience with tests, nor were there any extant tests appropriate for selecting men with aptitude for air combat in any position. I quote
my husband's views:

> We made tests for air crew aptitudes, hundreds upon hundreds of them; and we
> tested the tests in the Anglo-American tradition of statistical prediction. We vali-
> dated against the criteria of pass–fail in the flying schools, and the navigator, bom-
> bardier, and gunnery schools, and thus lifted ourselves by our own bootstraps.
> We analyzed the factors in the correlations between tests and struggled to inter-
> pret them. But I, at least, have never achieved a promising hypothesis by means of
> factor-analysis. The so-called "spatial" abilities extracted from the existing tests
> still seem to me unintelligible. The fact is, I now think, that the spatial perfor-
> mances of men and animals are based on stimulus-information of a mathematical
> order that we did not dream of in the 1940's. There are invariants of structure or
> pattern under transformation. (J. J. Gibson, 1967, p. 136)

James thought that he could do better with motion picture tests, which would
at least present the transformations over time as a plane moved and incorpo-
rate some of the information given in motion. I return to this topic later.

As the year advanced, the war picture looked bleaker and the house we
rented was sold, forcing us to move to a greatly inferior one. But there were
one or two bright spots. The new rented house had the advantage of being
only a few doors from our friends the Sollenbergers, and I found that I was
pregnant. From a personal point of view, it seemed to me a good time to have
another baby, when I could devote my time to my family without conflicts.
Keeping house was not simple, either, because of the gasoline rationing and
many food items that were in short supply. We were grateful, however, to be
together and to have pleasant company among our colleagues. Our daughter,
Jean, was born June 29, 1943, much to our delight. She throve, despite the
very hot weather. It was particularly hard on the children, because there was a
polio epidemic that summer, and the swimming pool was closed.

The Aviation Psychology Program at Fort Worth was not thriving, however.
Doubtless, it should have been located at some air base, rather than in the middle
of a big city. My husband was pleased when he was assigned to head a so-called

Psychological Test Film Unit that would be located at the Santa Ana Army Air Base in California, with access to a motion picture studio in Culver City. The thought of another move across the country, this time with two small children, was rather daunting, but California might be an improvement on Texas. My husband soon went ahead, driving with a friend, leaving me to pack up and bring the children after he had found a place to live.

I set out by train for California when Jean was 3 months old. We had a section in an ancient Pullman car, with an even more ancient porter (the young ones were all in the service and he had been summoned back from retirement). The trip took 3 days and was a nightmare. I describe only one incident. Our first night out, I put Jerry, who had sprained an ankle just before leaving, in the lower berth and took the baby into the upper with me. Jerry was apparently lonesome and a little frightened behind the curtains by himself and eventually began crying softly. The old porter heard him and came to his rescue. The curtains parted and my 3-year-old son was handed up to me. "This little boy wants to be with his mama," said the old porter, closing the curtains. After that night, the three of us slept (or tried to) in the lower berth.

My husband, now glorified to major's rank, met the train in Los Angeles and we were packed into our own old car and driven to a house he had rented in Santa Ana. It was a new bungalow, built where orange groves used to grow. There were still five orange trees in the yard. His mother had

Fig. 8. The Psychological Test Film Unit (from left to right): Lt. Ralph Eisenberg, Capt. George Lehner, Capt. James Gibson, and Lt. Robert Gagné.

come, too, to help us get settled—just as well, because the baby had a cold and a fever by that time. However, things soon settled down. Our neighbors in the other new bungalows mostly worked in aircraft factories, except for an elderly lady in a one-time farmhouse across the street. She was a bonus, because she was a kindly person and would babysit. We made a few friends among the military there, including Lloyd Humphreys, another psychologist, and his family, as well as the personnel in my husband's unit at the air base.

The Psychological Test Film Unit consisted of four officers and a number of enlisted men. Besides my husband, the officers were Capt. George Lehner and Lt. Robert Gagné, both young psychologists, and Lt. Ralph Eisenberg, a Hollywood type who knew, presumably, about the motion picture industry. Gagné had been a senior at Yale when my husband taught a small class there earlier. He had since acquired a PhD in psychology at Brown University, and my husband, finding his name among the available newly recruited psychologists, fortunately secured his help. They performed a number of experiments together, eventually, and he and his young wife, Pat, became our good friends. Alas, they did not live near us in Santa Ana, having found a small furnished house to rent on Balboa Island, normally a vacation spot but now filled with military personnel. I was stranded without transportation during the day, and the close neighbors, many of them recent arrivals from Oklahoma and other states, were at their wartime factory jobs. I spent my time with the children, reading to Jerry, taking the baby for walks in a second- (or third-)hand wicker carriage, and doing housework, including doing the laundry by hand, using a scrub-board to get the diapers clean. At least the warm California sun was great for drying them. In the evening I would hear about the work of my husband's unit, which was interesting, and make an occasional suggestion. Once or twice we had a party for the unit, which was a little like parties for graduate students in the prewar days. Some of the enlisted men in the unit were actually graduate students. Owing to rationing, the menu was limited, generally including baked beans and beer. They were cheerful gatherings, nevertheless.

The work of this unit has been written up in detail by my husband (a Lt. Colonel by the time he completed it) in a report to the Army Air Force and was published as a book *Motion Picture Testing and Research* (J. J. Gibson, 1947) by the U.S. Government Printing Office. Because the book is no longer in print and is doubtless not available in most libraries, I consider it appropriate (indeed important) to summarize some of its contents, which were completely novel at the time.

The mission of the unit was not only construction of motion picture tests for classification, but also research on methods of motion picture testing and training problems that were relevant for motion picture or other photographic techniques. The research part of the mission, of course, appealed particularly to James, an experimental and theoretical psychologist. The book includes in the first chapter "assumptions and hypotheses" that underlie the work. I cite one as an example, because it also typifies my husband's interest:

> The kind of behavior primarily involved in the task of flying is **locomotion in space** and on that account is extended in time. Hence, the performances required in flying are predominantly characterized by motion, by being continuous, and by possessing tempo. (J. J. Gibson, 1947, p. 5)

The majority of the tests produced were perceptual tests, as motion pictures have their most obvious application in this field. The research of the organization was divided into three parts: test development, training research, and problems of technique. The major objective, of course, was to construct motion picture tests for air crew classification purposes. The procedure would begin with a hypothesis regarding some function thought to be useful for prediction of success in one or more of the air crew duties: pilot, navigator, or bombardier. A test was then constructed and administered to a large group of aviation students and the test scores used to obtain the reliability of the test and its intercorrelation with other tests. Validity of the test was determined by correlating scores with success or failure in later phases of air crew training and performance. If the test satisfied the appropriate criteria, it could be included in the classification battery.

A large number of tests were constructed. I do not describe individual tests, but they were classifiable into the following areas:

1. Tests of ability to judge motion and locomotion, including judgment of visual motion (velocity and relative velocity), and one requiring judgment of one's own motion during simulated flight, presumably information needed for landing an airplane.
2. Tests of ability to judge distance.
3. Tests for orientation in space (maintaining orientation after a series of turns, and orientation in the traffic pattern).
4. Tests of ability to detect slight movement, presumably needed for synchronizing a bomb sight.
5. Tests requiring multiple perception, that is, alertness, and ability to keep diverse performance requirements in mind at the same time.

6. Tests involving sequential perception; These tests (using abstract figures) involved the ability to put successive partial impressions together in a complete figure. The figure to be perceived might be traced by a moving spot, or exposed a part at a time through a slot. (There have been numerous experiments on this phenomenon since that time.)
7. Tests of perceptual speed, using brief exposure intervals.
8. Tests of comprehension involving auditory-visual material presented by film, somewhat analogous to reading comprehension tests.

I have no idea how many of the tests were ultimately used in selection procedures, but the novelty of the material and the methods used made a lasting impression, both on psychologists and people involved in test construction. James's report includes meticulous description and illustration of the new methods. A number of proficiency tests were also constructed, including tests for aircraft recognition proficiency, navigation proficiency, and target identification for bombardiers.

Test construction, however, was not the only project to which the unit's efforts were devoted. One of the needs of all flying personnel at the time was the ability to recognize aircraft in the air, so as to discriminate between friendly planes and enemy planes, and to recognize the unique characteristics of each type. Such identification had to be taught, and taught well. The Psychological Test Film Unit was asked to perform research on how such identification was best learned, because it seemed reasonable that photography and perhaps shots of aircraft in motion would be useful for teaching. I was pleased at the time to hear about the project. It involved perceptual learning, and my dissertation research had given me ideas about principles that might be involved. My husband indeed cited my dissertation in his report and wrote, "As a basis for the experiment, it was therefore assumed that recognition training is essentially a kind of perceptual learning in which visual shapes not at the outset distinctive become capable of producing differential reactions" (J. J. Gibson, 1947, P. 120).

Many methods of training to eliminate confusion and help make the individual planes distinctive were tried, including photographs, slides given "flash presentations," models, motion pictures, silhouettes, teaching of distinctive unique features, constructing drawings, presentations of a plane in numerous aspects and at varying distances, and so on. Accuracy of recognition at maximum distances (allowing preparation for ensuing action) was a major criterion for successful training.

Many experiments comparing methods were done, including one testing the value of rapid flash speeds—a hitherto popular method, but one that proved to be of little value. The experiment I found most interesting compared practice in learning to identify "total forms" of planes with practice in which instruction emphasized "distinctive features." The total form groups probably discovered some distinctive features for themselves during training, but results showed a difference in favor of the feature-training group. It was concluded that effective training in aircraft recognition should emphasize the features that distinguish similar planes from each other. Time was thought to have been wasted emphasizing some unimportant features rather than stressing the distinguishing features of confusable planes. Such a prediction followed directly from my doctoral dissertation.

In another experiment, students were asked to draw planes as they would appear from three views, making single line drawings of silhouette shape. When these drawings were scored and correlated with ability to identify them by differential responses, a significant correlation was found. Composite drawings, made by superposing outlines on one another, were found to be in high agreement with outlines of each plane's real silhouette. The students had evidently learned to "visualize" each plane as unique as well as to respond to them differentially. Actually, the principal distinctive features were apt to be exaggerated, occasionally even caricatured. Other experiments showed that active differential responding with correction, as opposed to mere opportunity for passive association, was markedly superior.

Perhaps the most interesting and valuable portion of the report, a chapter titled "Perception and Judgment of Aerial Space and Distance as Potential Factors in Pilot Selection and Training," includes an analysis of stimulus variables that inform the perception of "space", and tests or experiments conducted on these variables. The first thing that had to be done was to redefine the concept of space, as aerial space must be distinguished from the space in a room or in the kind of pictorial situation that had traditionally been used in psychological laboratories. The kind of distance perception required for flying over a continuous space is entirely different from the kind one views with a stereoscope, in a small room, or in a pictured scene. One general statement can be made, however, that was fundamental to James Gibson's work from that time on. As he stated it in his report:

> The problem of three-dimensional vision, or distance perception, is basically a problem of a *continuous surface* which is seen to extend away from the observer. All spaces in which we can live include at least one surface, the ground or terrain. If there were no surface, there would be no visual world, strictly speaking. Whether we stand on it or fly over it, the ground is the basis of visual space perception both literally and figuratively. (J. J. Gibson, 1947, P. 185)

No one had said this before, and I believe that this basic assumption changed the whole future of research on and understanding of so-called space perception. Distance does not consist of a theoretical line extending outward from the eye to an object, but is rather defined by the surface or substratum that extends away from us. The sky is not a surface and therefore the distance of a plane seen simply against the sky is correspondingly difficult to estimate.

Gibson proceeded to list and discuss the stimulus variables that could make possible the perception of a continuous surface. There must be, he suggested, retinal gradients of stimulation. These included gradients of texture (as in a plowed field); gradients of size of similar objects; gradients of velocity during movement of the observer providing, along with texture of the background, a gradient of "motion perspective", beginning with a maximum at the points of the terrain nearest the observer and ending with zero movement at the horizon; gradients arising from atmospheric transmission of light (so-called aerial perspective); and a retinal gradient of binocular disparity (not simply disparity as such).

Fig. 9.   Test of proficiency of distance estimation—Judgment of
size-at-a-distance (Figure 9.5 from J. Gibson, 1947, Army Air Forces
Aviation Psychology Program Research Reports: Motion Picture Testing
and Research, Report No. 7, p. 202).

Psychophysical experiments were designed to explore these variables using motion pictures when feasible. These experiments are described in some detail in the 1947 report. I include an illustration from one of them that is very well known, a test for judging size at a distance (Gibson, 1947, p. 202). The situation was set up in a stretch of level ground (a field of cultivated land). Near stakes were set in the ground at 14 yards from the observer, and the distant stake (of variable size) was set at six different distances, the farthest at 784 yards. The observer was to match the variable, distant stake to one of the set of 15 near stakes. An experiment was run in the open air, and in addition, a photographic repetition was made of all conditions of the experiment. The average error made in judging the size of the test stake turned out to be relatively small, even when the test stake was far away. The accuracy of perception was reduced in photographs as compared with real space, and variability increased, not surprisingly. The most interesting thing about this experiment is what it reveals about perceptual size constancy. Apparent size of the target stake remained constant up to a point where the object was only barely visible. "Constancy is simply the rule," J. J. Gibson (1947, p. 211) said. Objects on the terrain do not appear to be smaller than they actually are, as the distance is increased, although judgments may become more variable. Accuracy declined with distance, but not constancy. The old method (once actually in use) of moving things away from the observer to make them appear at a greater distance was simply incorrect, because their size was still detectable.

I should mention one other test because of the novelty of the underlying concept. This was a test of the ability to judge distance in terms of the "retinal motion cue." Retinal displacement occurs when an object is seen to move across the field of view. But when the observer moves, the entire field is deformed. As James phrased it:

> The general rule may be formulated that when the *observer himself* moves, the retinal image corresponding to the whole visual field undergoes deformation. The converse is also true. When the observer's body is motionless, there is *no* deformation of the retinal image as a whole.

> When objects move, the corresponding object-images within the retinal image of the field undergo relative displacement (and may also undergo deformation if the objects move toward or away from us) but the retinal background-image of the whole field does not undergo deformation. This rule holds even though the eyes may move from one fixation to another or may fixate a moving object, *so long as the head does not move*, i.e., so long as the *position* of the eyes in space does not change.

When *both* the observer and objects move in a three-dimensional space, there occurs both deformation of the retinal background-image and displacement (possibly with deformation) of the retinal object-images. Both the observer's own movement and the movement of objects are perceived simultaneously, under normal circumstances, without any interference between the two kinds of perception. (J. J. Gibson, 1947, p. 220)

This extraordinarily important fact is now well known to all perception psychologists, but it had never hitherto been noted. Even human infants as early as 4 or 5 months old have been shown to differentiate between the visual results of their own displacement and that of concurrent motion of an object (Kellman, Gleitman, & Spelke, 1987).

The deformation of the total retinal image with observer motion was later referred to by Gibson as "optic flow" and was referred to in his work at that time as "retinal motion perspective." To make the perspective information clear, James constructed diagrams that have since been reproduced in dozens of volumes on space perception. I include two of them here.

It is a fact that "the velocity of the retinal flow approaches zero for very distant objects, and vanishes at two specific points in the visual world—the point toward which the observer is moving and its opposite, the point he is moving away from" (J. J. Gibson, 1947, p. 221). James noted that the expansion pattern could be noticed when driving a car on a straight road, and the corresponding contraction observed from the rear end of a train (something he had often done).

I do not go into detailed discussion about how these changes in the optic array inform us about the changing distances of surfaces and objects as we move, as the explanation is presented in more recent, available volumes (e.g., J. J. Gibson, 1950, 1966, and others). The point here is that these discoveries were used to construct a motion picture test for accuracy of judgment during landing an airplane. Motion pictures taken of the expansion patterns during landing and gliding were realistic and "gave an onlooker a compelling experience of being moved toward the ground in a slanting path" (J. J. Gibson, 1947, p. 230) although the camera field was restricted as compared with actual viewing. A test of landing judgment was constructed on 16-mm sound film and administered to 1,200 cadets. Validity ratings could not be determined by the Test Film Unit at the time, and I do not know what use was finally made of the test. What I have stressed here is the creative thinking and serious problem solving that resulted in novel techniques and some totally new views on how space is perceived. Fortunately, James was able to ponder them at length and present them in a later book after the war's end (J. J. Gibson, 1950).

Fig. 10. Diagrams of optic flow [Figures 9.8 (ahead), and 9.12 (landing) from J. J. Gibson, 1947, Army Air Forces Aviation Psychology Program Research Reports: Motion Picture Testing and Research Report No. 7, pp. 222, 227].

I have given only a minimal account of the work that went on at Santa Ana in the Test Film Unit. The family was having its problems in the meantime. The comfortable bungalow in Santa Ana, where Jean learned to walk and in fact to climb on a jungle gym in the backyard before she was 2 years old, was sold to Los Angeles people who had prospered during the war. This was a serious problem for us, because the housing shortage had become acute, to put it mildly. The day of our enforced move approached, and we had found no place to move to. I could have taken the children to Illinois and waited out the rest of the war at my mother's home in Peoria, but I was reluctant to do that. Just a few days before our enforced removal, the Air Force Emergency Relief Office called and said an officer's home in Corona del Mar was available for 1 month. The officer (absent and on duty) was a regular Army man and had a beach house there, unneeded at the moment.

This was a tremendous piece of luck for us, and by the time the month was up, it was fall, and we found a tiny vacation house to rent on Balboa Island. The house at Corona del Mar was wonderful. It faced the ocean, only a road between the house and a steep path down to a beach. It was minimally furnished, but that didn't matter. Friends who could manage the gasoline loved to come call, climb down the steep path, and swim in the ocean. I took the children down to the beach every day, carrying Jean and sliding part way. Of course they loved it. One morning I went to the room the children shared to get them up, and found Jean's crib empty. I asked Jerry, who was calmly perusing a comic book in bed, where she was. "Oh," he said, "she went to the beach." I dashed across the road, and there she was, halfway down the steep path, maneuvering it with great agility, in night clothes and wet diaper. I persuaded her back, promising a later visit. Jerry, meanwhile, had started kindergarten (in Santa Ana) and continued there as September came. There wasn't much for him to learn academically, but he grew accustomed to a morning with other children in a pretty diverse group, and learned about riding on school buses. He had plenty of books at home.

In the fall we moved to Balboa Island (truly an island, with a paved walk all the way around it). It was packed with small vacation houses, and we enjoyed it, crowded or not. We stayed there until we finally left for home, in the early summer of 1946. James was kept there after the war ended to write his book-length history of the Test Film Unit.

I have not mentioned one serendipitous consequence of our wartime residence in California. A group of the Gibson relatives lived around Los Angeles, and they were eager to see us, especially the children. Aunt Cad and Aunt Mildred (my father-in-law's sisters) lived together in a very large apartment in Los Angeles. Aunt Cad was a widow and Aunt Mildred a retired spinster who had been a successful businesswoman and still managed their considerable wealth. Uncle Link (their brother-in-law) lived on a small ranch not far away, with his daughter Fern and granddaughter Jesslyn. His wife had died recently, and Fern was a widow, so they had become a very close family group. We were invited to their ranch on a Sunday not long after our arrival in Santa Ana and drove there for lunch. I had never met any of them before, but they were extremely cordial and I liked them all. After that, we went every couple of months to see the aunts in Los Angeles, and in fact attended Jesslyn's wedding before we left for home. James's brother Tom and his wife came all the way from San Francisco for it, so it was quite a family reunion.

It was too late to go back in time to teach by the time James was released from the Air Force, so we took our time driving back across the country, stopping at interesting and beautiful places. One of the places we stopped was the Grand Canyon, and the children both danced around on the rim, making me nervous (but I would have been any way—heights distress me). My husband reminded me that they could see the depth as well as I could, and I believed him. Contrary to a popular myth, this occasion was not the inspiration for my later research on the visual cliff. We stopped in Illinois, too, of course, and visited both grandmothers before finally reaching our home in Northampton, now vacated by its wartime inhabitants.

Smith was taking me back after a 4-year leave. What a wonderful institution! I was a little worried about possible rustication of my teaching skills, and even more about proper child care while I was occupied, but things worked out well.

5

Back to Civilization
(Academic Style)

We returned joyfully to our beloved house in Northampton and spent some time getting things unpacked and reorganized and setting rooms up properly for the children; two rooms were needed now! We also needed to prepare a room for a live-in helper. Before we left California, my husband had met the relocation director for the Japanese people who had been sent to internment camps during the war. He had been superintendent of one of the camps, and was well acquainted with the internees. He told my husband of a young woman (17 years old) who had been a babysitter for his family and needed to be placed somewhere. She had just finished high school (at the camp) before the internees were released. The people at his camp included mainly Japanese citizens who had lost their small farm plots in California and now had nowhere to go. Many of them were being sent to New Jersey, where a Seabrook canning factory was hiring a number of employees. This girl's family had gone there, but it did not seem an auspicious place for a bright young person. The relocation director recommended her highly and gave us their new address in New Jersey.

I wrote to her, Sadako Okamoto, explaining who we were, describing the family, and informing her that we needed a trustworthy young person who would live with us as one of the family and help with the children. We would pay her, of course, and we would also help her to get on with her education. She wrote back eager to come. Her parents spoke only Japanese, so I could not communicate with them, but they obviously wanted her to leave the canning factory, where she still had only Japanese neighbors and no apparent opportunities. So, one day early in September we left the children with friends and drove to New Jersey to get Sadako (known to us ever after, even now, as Sadie, her preferred nickname).

Sadie, nicely dressed in a gray suit, was an attractive young woman, lively and friendly. We met her parents, of course, at their trailer home. They were very polite and smiling, although we could not converse with them. We told her about our lives and schedules and about the children on the drive home, and she told us about her life in the camp, the school (no books for the students), and her ambitions. She wanted, above anything, to be a nurse. Part of the reason was that a registered nurse could join the armed forces and become a citizen. She had been born in Japan, and to our astonishment wanted desperately to be an American citizen. However, she would have to learn a lot to get into nursing school. Her written English was very poor. We promised to help her get the preparation that she needed.

Sadie and the children got on marvelously together from the moment they met. She treated them as she would her own younger siblings (she had two brothers), loving them but making them mind their manners. Everyone settled in. Jerry went to first grade at the Smith College Day School, and Jean to the college's preschool program in the mornings. These were both run by Smith's Education Department and were pleasant and effective enough, although a little permissive for our taste. Sadie went several evenings a week to an English class at the People's Institute, an endowed Northampton institution where college students volunteered to teach and many classes were offered. I did all the cooking at first, but Sadie was eager to learn and soon helped with that, and shared other housework with me. We were incredibly fortunate that this arrangement worked out so well. I had enough time for my job, and we had a very pleasant family life as well, with a big sister for the children.

James's youngest brother, Bill, had received a PhD in English from the University of Chicago and served in the armed forces during the war. He now had a position teaching English at Williams College, not very far from Northampton, to our great pleasure. He had married Barbara Crane, his professor's daughter. They had two children, the oldest, Julia, only a year or two younger than Jean. We enjoyed frequent visits with them until they moved to Montclair, New Jersey, when Bill became a professor at New York University (NYU). James's other brother, Tom, was a businessman, working for Stouffer Chemical Company in San Francisco. About the time that Bill moved to NYU, Tom's office was moved to New York, and he and his wife bought a home in Scarsdale. The three brothers now managed to get together regularly, and when we were all together, we had a wonderful time. It was good for the children to know all these close relatives, especially their cousins Julia and Tom.

My sister, Emily Jack, a graduate of Simmons College, went to Chicago at the start of World War II to work for the Office of Censorship. After 2 years, she transferred to the United Nations Relief and Rehabilitation Administration (UNRRA) and was sent overseas at the end of the fighting in Europe to work in the Displaced Persons Operation. She remained with UNRRA afterward in Washington, DC, writing up the history of the organization. When that was finished, she moved to the Central Intelligence Agency (CIA) and stayed for 30 years as an expert on Soviet energy and electricity generation. When she retired, she stayed in Washington, DC, still her home. We never knew exactly what she did at the CIA, but the children loved to tell their friends that their aunt was a spy! They knew her well, because she and my mother usually spent Christmas with us (as Emily still does). Both grandmothers were frequent visitors. Both were widows by 1941, but continued to live in Illinois.

Our lives in Northampton were not quite the same as in previous times. James no longer went in for theatricals or played at labor unions. We no longer went mountain climbing with friends, as we did before we had children. The theatricals went by the board primarily because James's hearing began to deteriorate seriously at this time, and also because he was determined to make his new discoveries about perception and the importance of motion information available to a larger psychological audience. It meant devoting his spare time to writing a book. We had good friends, of course: new next door neighbors with a child Jean's age, the Heider family just around the corner with three boys, old friends on the faculty, and of course our colleagues in the psychology department. Smith had a new president, Herbert Davis, again British, this time an English professor from Cornell.

My life became extremely busy, as I had a full teaching load as well as my household to run. The household ran very smoothly. Sadie settled in and helped with many things, but my job did not become less demanding. I taught two large sections of the introductory course, now offered without a lab.

Dropping the lab happened during my absence, and there was no longer one single, very large lecture section attended by all comers. Classes were handled individually and given by several faculty members. The classes had enrollments of about 40 students each, the course lasted two semesters, and the instructors made their own plans. I found that I regretted the absence of the laboratory, and spent a lot of time working up demonstrations for my classes. I have never been sure what is the best method of teaching the introductory course, nor am I now. A large lecture section accompanied by small sections taught by assistants or lesser members of a department is a favorite method, but the lecturer has to be nothing short of a wizard if the audience becomes very large as it does at Cornell, for example, with a course enrollment of nearly 2,000! Few departments have a member who wants to take on this job for more than a year or two. The more specialized advanced courses are always more satisfactory to teach, and more attractive and profitable for the students, too. I had the animal (now comparative) psychology course to teach, as well, but the rat lab had disappeared during my absence. I rather regretted that, too. I had other duties—committees, a few MA candidates, and so on—and found myself too busy to start any new research at that time. I told myself that the time would come, and again I got a lot of satisfaction, as I had during the war, by following my husband's work and having discussions with him. The children now tell me that they thought we were arguing! Sometimes we were.

My husband's professional life was decidedly fuller than mine at that time. His professional life and career were changing and his research and writing were of greater importance to him than they had been before the war. He was eager to follow up his new ideas about perception and set them forth in a book written for psychologists, with the ambition of turning around the static, structural view of perception that had dominated psychology ever since Titchener's time, kept in the light by Boring, Titchener's loyal student who ruled at Harvard and over the Experimentalists. The psychology of learning, my particular interest, had turned toward functionalism (by way of behaviorism), but perception still seemed pretty much where Titchener had left it. As soon as James had settled down, he began his book, to be called *Perception of the Visual World*. It would throw out elementarism, emphasize the importance of real, everyday perceptual contact with the world, and include his arguments and the evidence for a dynamic, realistic view of perception, a radical enterprise at that time. There was much to say that was new.

Leonard Carmichael, the editor of the series in which the book was published, wrote a cautious introduction:

The student will find in this volume an interesting discussion of the old and difficult problem of the nature of visual depth. The author also deals with the constancy and characteristics of perceived objects in relation to geometric space and many other related topics. (J. J. Gibson, 1950, p. v)

Contrast this with a related statement taken from James's own preface:

A theoretical approach is called for because the perception of what has been called space is the basic problem of all perception. We perceive a world whose fundamental variables are spatial and temporal—a world which extends and endures. Space perception (from which time is inseparable) is not, therefore, a division of the subject matter of perception but the first problem to consider, without a solution for which other problems remain unclear. (J. J. Gibson, 1950, p. vii)

This view was expanded as he presented his theoretical approach:

The basic idea is that visual space should be conceived not as an object or an array of objects in air but as a continuous surface or an array of adjoining surfaces. The spatial character of the visual world is given not by the objects in it but by the background of the objects. It is exemplified by the fact that the airplane pilot's space, paradoxical as it may seem, is determined by the ground and the horizon, not by the air through which he flies. (J. J. Gibson, 1950, p. 6)

James called his view a "ground theory" of space perception. He thought that stimulus variables in the form of gradients would be found for surfaces and edges. At that time he looked for them in correlates in the retinal image. He suggested discarding the old distinction between sensation and perception, substituting instead the terms *visual field* and *visual world*. It was, of course, the visual world that interested him, although he wrote about the visual field as well. Introspecting on it required a very analytic, nonobjective attitude. The notion got him into trouble, but he wanted, at the time, to write about patterns of stimulation on the retina, hoping to find correlates for his gradients there. It remains a useful discussion, because it includes the first serious discussions of occlusion, of deformations produced by movement, and of the potential correlates of constancy. The correlates suggested were new to psychophysics, including texture gradients and abrupt discontinuities. These were all magnificently illustrated in the book (as Boring commented in his review of the book).

He was especially concerned, as a result of his wartime research, with the perception of distance and the stimulus correlates for it. The gradient underlying the perceived surface extending away had to begin with *here*, here being specified in the visual field by the vague image of the nose. The most novel discussions are found in the chapter on the active observer and the chapters following in which James showed how, despite movement of the observer, the world observed remains perceptually stable. Stimulus variables available to the active observer were discussed in detail, making full use of the knowledge he had acquired from his experiences in the Army Air Force and his Psychological Test Film Unit. The gradients of optical flow produced by the pilot's (observer's) movement are presented in full detail, explaining exactly what happens to the gradients as different maneuvers are performed. A nice example is the diagram of a "landing glide" (J. J. Gibson, 1950, p. 128), a figure often reproduced.

In discussing the perceived stability of the world even as visual stimulation is shifting with our movement, James presented a hypothesis that has been accepted ever since, with some conceptual and linguistic corrections that he later made:

> Moreover, a series of transformations can be endlessly and gradually applied to a pattern without affecting its invariant properties. The retinal image of a moving observer would be an example of this principle. Perhaps the clue we are seeking lies in the invariant properties of such a continually changing retinal image. Only these properties would be capable of providing the stimulus basis for a stable and unchanging world. (J. J. Gibson, 1950, p. 154)

As the story proceeds, it becomes even clearer that only stimulation considered over time will yield the invariant properties that are required for accurate perception of a real world.

One of the contributions of *The Perception of the Visual World* was its discussion of object constancy, the fact that objects look much the same size at different distances from the observer, and the same shape at different angles of regard or from different points of view, despite changes in the retinal image. Is this because we "know" the size or shape and "correct" our sensations? James said no, that the problem of constancy is only one aspect of the larger problem of how we perceive the visual world with *all* of its objective characteristics. He showed, in his discussion, that constancy actually has a basis in stimulation if concomitant and reciprocal stimuli are considered as joint variables, and if stimulation is taken as occurring over time. His gradient theory, plus concomitant stimulation, could handle the problem. Knowing, as we do nowadays, that very young infants perceive objects as constant in size, we can discard the old version as an explanation. An object is perceived simultaneously as an object at a certain distance and as having a shape at a given orientation. Multidimensional information occurs in perceptual arrays (although *Perception of the Visual World* did not use this terminology). For objects to be perceived as constant in size, they must be perceived as grounded on a visible surface.

The importance of grounding occurred to James very late one evening, and he immediately thought of a demonstration to prove it. Two objects of the same size would be shown with the same background surface, one actually resting on the surface and the other raised (invisibly) above it, so that it appeared to be grounded at a different distance. The objects would appear to be the same size when one was raised higher and placed nearer, because the height would appear to ground it farther away. He called to me and asked, "Do we have anything in the house, like a tablecloth, that has a very regular pattern that I could use for a background?"

I rummaged around and found a blanket of oblong pieces of wool (cut from old suits) that his mother had crocheted together with a lighter shade of wool. Perfect! We hastened to the lab and set up the demonstration. It worked, of course, and the next day we took pictures of it.

I have just been reading James's chapter on perceiving meanings. In places it comes close to his later concept of perceiving affordances (e.g. such statements as "food looks eatable, shoes look wearable," etc.) but it never quite gets there. He stated that it was an oversimplification that "all meaning is learned," thereby anticipating a raging present-day controversy. He made a distinction between spatial meanings and verbal meanings. He pointed out that among animals there is good evidence for innately meaningful perceptions, but the human animal matures slowly and learns much more than other species. With the little evidence at his disposal at that time, he thought that perhaps "the human infant does not begin to learn meanings at a zero level" (J. J. Gibson, 1950, p. 208). We cannot speak with much greater certainty even now, although we are aware of the huge importance of perceptual learning in infancy for learning meanings of things and events. The chapter on learning finishes prophetically, "The progress of learning is from indefinite to definite, not from sensation to perception" (p. 222). Together, the two of us expanded on that statement several years later.

It is particularly interesting to note that the last chapter in this book, written 50 years ago, brings in the ego, a very modern topic: "Perceiving the world has an observer aspect, perceiving oneself." In his later books, James made much more of this topic, but he described here a number of "forms of stimulation which might yield a primitive ego in perception" (J. J. Gibson, 1950, p. 224). This conclusion predates by many years his friend Ulric Neisser's "ecological self" (Neisser, 1988).

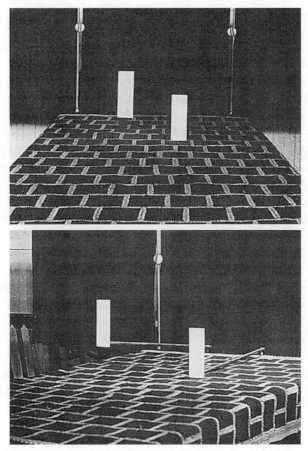

Fig. 11. Demonstration of perceived distance as dependent on contact with
a background (Figure 72 from J. J. Gibson, 1950, The Perception of the
Visual World, Houghton Mifflin, p. 179).

Most of the views expressed in this book were very radical at the time, but
on the whole, it was favorably received, and certainly guaranteed the author
a place among the major experimental psychologists of the time. The importance of gradients of stimulation for guiding locomotion was generally recognized as a major insight, especially the gradient of texture on surfaces. When
the book appeared, it was reviewed by Boring for the *Psychological Bulletin*,
the major book review journal. Boring's review was decidedly favorable in
tone, despite the book's fundamental departure from his own ideas. He began the review thus:

In these stern days of harsh, quantitative statisticized psychophysics it is with surprise that one turns up so fresh, so clear, so stimulating, and so unquantitative a phenomenology as is Gibson's scholarly description of what we see and how we see. (Boring, 1951, p. 360)

He went on to praise its 81 figures as "magnificently good," and to point out its emphasis on relationships and invariants. "All in all," he concluded, "the reviewer finds this book a remarkably keen, clear and wise description of just how it is that people see things" (p. 363). However, in his long review, Boring also criticized Gibson's distinction between the visual field and the visual world as being unclear and later wrote short critiques of it (Boring, 1952, 1953). Gibson answered them (J. J. Gibson, 1952). It is not clear who won, however, because Gibson later (J. J. Gibson, 1966) gave up the distinction. But Boring's (1951) insistence on distinguishing sensation and perception had an uneasy future, too. The book's reception on the whole was good, however. Hochberg (1990) wrote that the 1950 book remains influential: "I found some 500 citations for *Perception of the Visual World* since 1979" (p.751). It was undoubtedly this book that inspired the Society of Experimental Psychologists, in 1952, to award to James their prestigious Howard Crosby Warren Medal.

As the book neared completion, James became more and more eager to work with graduate students who would be interested in pursuing research on the many new hypotheses he was introducing. He was restless at Smith and began to listen as hints of jobs at major universities reached us. One day, I asked him, "Where would you really like to go?" He answered, "Cornell, I think." The very next day, he received an offer from Cornell. The coincidence was staggering but real.

The Cornell University Psychology Department had a new chairman, Robert B. McLeod. He had come from McGill University, where he had remade their department and had gained a reputation for rebuilding departments that needed strengthening. He himself was interested in perception, and he wanted Cornell's department to be the strongest in the country in that field. He invited James as full professor, and also Julian Hochberg, a new PhD who was prophesied as being a coming leader in the field. Both accepted. The department also had T. A. Ryan, a Cornell PhD, who had been brought up in the old Cornell tradition of perception, but was a wise and open-minded scholar. The new perception group was indeed strong.

Cornell University had a nepotism rule, and thus offered me no position. I was sure that we should go, in any case, and that I would find some opportunity for getting back to research, which I had no time for at Smith. The decision was right, and I did do research for many years thereafter, though I surely did not anticipate just how varied it would be.

Sadie, after spending 3 postwar years with us, had just been accepted for nurse's training, so we all looked forward to a new future. We moved to Cornell in the fall of 1949, and James's book, *Perception of the Visual World*, came out in early 1950.

6

High Above
Cayuga's Waters

Cornell University stands on hills above Lake Cayuga, one of New York's Finger Lakes, and has a wonderful prospect from the side of the campus that overlooks the lake. Not only that, two very deep gorges run through the campus. One borders the campus on its south side, dividing it from College Town, a collection of small shops, restaurants, and rather tacky apartment buildings housing graduate students. The other borders the north side, dividing the campus from Cayuga Heights, a residential district inhabited mainly by professors and their families. There is a car bridge over both gorges, and also, farther down each gorge, a swinging foot bridge from which one can peer down at the rocks and water far below while crossing. The campus is further divided by an imaginary line in the other direction into the lower campus (on the lakeside) and the upper campus above it. The lower campus houses the College of Arts and Sciences, the College of Architecture, the main library, the art museum, and the Law School, which are privately endowed. The upper campus houses the College of Agriculture, the Veterinary College, the College of Home Economics (now renamed the College of Human Ecology), a second library, and several other schools, all part of the State University of New York. Ezra Cornell, when he founded the University, wanted it to be an institution where one could study any subject, and that is just about true. A renowned president of Cornell in the 1890s, Andrew Dickson White, had publicly attacked organized religion and praised science, so all the schools, endowed and state alike, were strong in science.

The Psychology Department is part of the College of Arts and Sciences, but there is also a Department of Human Development and Family Relations in the College of Human Ecology that includes a number of psychologists. There are psychologists scattered about in the other schools, too, such as the School of Labor and Industrial Relations (a state school), and of course in the Medical School, which is in New York City. Cornell has a very beautiful campus, and as diversified a group of scholars as one could find. The atmosphere was, definitely, very congenial to us.

Our first year there, we rented an apartment in a newly built complex on the edge of Cayuga Heights called Lakeland Homes. It was a short trip to campus, and the children could walk to the Cayuga Heights School, a small school with a reputation for excellent and devoted teachers. Our neighbors in the apartments were mostly newcomers like ourselves, or visiting faculty, a number of them European or Asian. We soon made friends there because there were many children who quickly found each other. Jean began first grade and Jerry went to fifth grade. There he made friends with boys in his grade, especially one who lived nearby whose father was dean of the College of Agriculture and another whose father was a professor in the Law School. Jean made many friends, especially one, Diana Hall, whose father, a linguist, later found me a copy of "Integer Vitae" when I needed it for a memorial service. Our apartment, though pleasant, was a little cramped and we looked for a house in Cayuga Heights, eventually finding one which we inhabited for 30 years, remodeled several times, and came to love, although it could not match the beauty of our old Northampton house.

I had hoped that I would find opportunities for research at Cornell and I did, in a most unexpected quarter. Because I was not a member of the faculty, I had no laboratory of my own and needed an invitation to work in someone else's. Professor Howard Liddell, a member of the Psychology Department, offered me a job doing research at his laboratory, known as the "Behavior Farm." Liddell was a well-known behaviorist; not only that, his research was focused on the experimental neurosis, a phenomenon (if such it really was) at that time in vogue. He was very generously supported by the

Rockefeller Foundation and was ruler of a large farm maintaining herds of sheep and goats, and an ample laboratory housed in a one-time barn now furnished with a meeting room, laboratory rooms, and elaborate equipment. The equipment was set up for conditioning the subjects (sheep or goats) to the sound of a buzzer or bell, and shocking them on a foot or foreleg. The hypothesis was that conditioning with inescapable shock, day after day, would make the helpless subject neurotic. The animals' responses were carefully monitored, including breathing and heart rate. There were barrels full of records of breathing and heart rate sitting around (I suspected unread). I was suspicious of the presumed neurotic condition of the experimental subjects, but it was an opportunity to work with animals, which I had always wanted to do, and I felt sure I could work into some problem of my own. I did, and I describe the work later. My career there was short (2 years), and although in some ways bizarre, it was rewarding and broadening.

The Cornell Psychology Department at the time was crowded into the two top floors of Morrill Hall, one of the old, original buildings. There were magnificent views of the lake from upper windows, but space was at a premium. Nevertheless, there were a number of graduate students of high quality, and James soon had his share of them. They all referred to him as J. J. (and to me as Mrs. G.). It was a very happy department, busy with research and colloquia, with real communication and informality. The full professors in experimental psychology included R. B. McLeod, T. A. Ryan, H. Liddell, and J. J. Gibson. Younger faculty were J. Hochberg (perception) and Kay Montgomery (learning, also new). There were others (senior and junior) in statistics, testing, personality, social psychology, and so on, whom I remember less well, except for one, Patricia Smith, also a newcomer, who taught industrial psychology. I believe she was one of the first women to be appointed to the faculty of the Arts College or at least to make professor (which she eventually did). Pat was married to Olin Smith, a young man who had just finished his degree in psychology. Because Pat was appointed to the faculty, her husband could not be, and was in my position, seeking a job elsewhere or looking for a research position. This couple (childless and younger than we were) became our fast friends.

Other good friends were the MacLeods and the Ryans. Both families had children the ages of ours, and in both cases the wives, Beatrice MacLeod and Mary Ryan, were professional women. Bea McLeod taught theater at Ithaca College, which included staging productions several times a year, a career that interested my husband especially. He no longer acted, partly because he was becoming increasingly deaf, but also because his heart was in his developing theory of perception and he put all his energy into that. Mary Ryan had a PhD in psychology from Cornell, as was her husband's. She had just been offered a position teaching "psychology of clothing" in the Cornell College of Home Economics. This appointment was not considered a case of nepo-tism, because the college was a different one, in the state-supported part of the university. I could not imagine what psychology one would teach in a course in clothing. Perhaps she couldn't either, and had to make it up from scratch. But it seemed no stranger to her than my job of doing research on sheep and goats. However, my job was what I wanted, a chance to get my hand in at research again, and I became more and more interested in the op-portunities and new research questions that I saw opening up. I could ar-range my own hours, too. Jean came home from school for lunch, and I would dash home at noon, shed my farm clothes (blue jeans, which I hung out the window), and prepare lunch. She occasionally said, "Mother, you smell like a goat" (probably true).

By the end of our first year at Cornell, we had found a house in Cayuga Heights, just a block beyond the apartments, at 111 Oak Hill Road. It was a white stucco house, probably one of the earliest built in the Heights. It had a pleasant living room, a large study, dining room, and kitchen downstairs. Up-stairs were four bedrooms (one very tiny, where I worked in the evenings) and just one bathroom. There was a barnlike two-car garage that had an up-stairs, to the children's delight. I can't imagine why, unless the original owner taught in the College of Agriculture and fancied some sort of barn. Its upstairs had several large windows and became a favorite place for the children to play. What pleased us most was the back yard, which was very large, slop-ing upward gently, well wooded with old cherry trees, and no buildings in sight at the end of it. It was a beautiful yard. The house had a covered brick terrace in back that looked out on the yard. We held Jean's wedding there years later, a perfect place for it.

The opportunities for James's research proved to be everything he had hoped. Space was cramped, but he got his labs and, most important, won-derful colleagues and graduate students. I name a few of the earlier ones: Howard Flock, Horace Reynolds, George Kaplan, Kirk Wheeler, Jean Purdy, Rick Warren, and others, whose names may be found as co-authors on research publications. He started a weekly Thursday afternoon seminar on perception, attended by graduate students and some faculty, where deep problems were argued. Visitors began to come from elsewhere, some from Europe. He developed the habit of preparing and handing out ahead of time a few paragraphs, formulating the question for discussion for the day and some very provocative possible answers to it. These remarks were copied on a ditto machine in purple ink, and became known as "purple perils."

There were hundreds of them by 1979, the year of James's death. Friends have now collected, copied, and bound them, and made them available on the Internet. A few of them were published in *Reasons for Realism* (1982), a collection of essays by James edited by Edward Reed and Rebecca Jones.

The focus of James's early research at Cornell was on surface perception, especially the information for a surface, including information obtained from motion. Experiments were soon set up to check out the new hypotheses, involving graduate students in the projects. One performed with Walter Carel suggests the new trend in perceptual research, "Does Motion Perspective Independently Produce the Impression of a Receding Surface?" (J. J. Gibson & Carel, 1952). James also found colleagues in mathematics and engineering at Cornell, and got two of them interested in devising mathematical expressions of the information for depth in motion for an observer aiming at a target. Their discussions resulted in a paper, "Parallax and Perspective During Aircraft Landings" (J. J. Gibson, Olum, & Rosenblatt, 1955).

An important event in those early years at Cornell was a symposium on perception arranged by McLeod and Gibson. There was an International Conference of Psychology at Montreal in early June, 1954. Naturally, the Cornell psychologists attended, and so did many European psychologists. A number of prominent psychologists who were interested in perception were invited to Cornell for discussions following the Montreal meeting. The symposium went on for nearly a week, proceeding informally with contributions from all the members. The participants included Egon Brunswik (University of California at Berkeley), James Drever (University of Edinburgh), James J. Gibson (Cornell University), Fritz Heider (University of Kansas), Julian Hochberg (Cornell University), Gunnar Johansson (Uppsala University, Sweden), George Klein (New York University), Ivo Kohler (University of Innsbruck, Austria), Robert McLeod (Cornell University), Wolfgang Metzger (University of Munster, Germany), T. A. Ryan (Cornell University), and Hans Wallach (Swarthmore College). Albert Michotte (University of Louvain) had been invited as well, but was ill, unfortunately, and could not attend.

A report on the discussions was prepared by Julian Hochberg and published in the Psychological Review (Hochberg, 1957). He called his report "Effects of the Gestalt Revolution: The Cornell Symposium on Perception," but actually, there is little flavor of Gestalt psychology in the report and there were no confirmed Gestaltists among the participants, either the Americans or the Europeans. The interactions among participants were fruitful, and some new emphases for studying perception emerged. The necessity of studying perception of events over time; of seeking higher order variables that might lead to a "global psychophysics" instead of the old

Fig. 12. The Cornell Perception Symposium.

elementaristic psychophysical approach; and quite general agreement on a new law or principle, dubbed the Minimum Principle, essentially the view that perception is selective and will make use of the least, most economical information that serves to specify the event or situation perceived. (I may have rephrased the latter a bit to conform with my own ideas, as different members of the group had different phraseologies for it). Gunnar Johansson, who was just introducing to this country his work on motion perception, was very influential in reaching this conviction. It was also suggested that the study of perceptual learning was a critical and needy area. Ivo Kohler, introducing his experiments on adaptation to prisms, was certainly influential in pushing this suggestion.

The time of the participants was by no means devoted to all work and no play. Ithaca is very beautiful in early summer and there were picnics and parties. Our old friends the Heiders (Fritz, Grace, and one of their sons) stayed in our house with us. Grace and I, although both psychologists, were not invited to the discussions, but we dutifully assisted with the entertainment. One day we made potato salad for all (families included) for a picnic at Enfield Glen, one of the beautiful state parks in the area. On the last afternoon of the meeting, I held a farewell tea party in the Gibson back yard, inviting all the graduate students as well as participants and their families. It was a beautiful day and a splendid setting, a good finale for the occasion. I remember Hans Wallach, perched on a low tree branch, saying he had never enjoyed a party more.

It was not a finale for the friendships that were formed, however. My husband, in that week, established lifelong friendships with Gunnar Johansson and Ivo Kohler. It was by no means the last we saw of them, as I shall tell.

Now, however, I tell a little more about my own activities in the early years at Cornell. I have already mentioned that I was invited by Professor Liddell to assist with the research of his Behavior Farm, working with sheep and goats. His project was to study the so-called experimental neurosis, presumably established in animals by a classical conditioning procedure using shock as the reinforcer. A signal such as a buzzer or change in lighting was followed by a shock to the foot that could not be escaped. After numerous repetitions of this procedure, the animals' breathing and heart rate was indeed disturbed in the experimental setup. I doubted that this was truly neurotic behavior, as I watched the animals vainly struggling while I continued the prescribed experimental regimen. In any case, I was not particularly interested in the experimental neurosis and I set out to explore another problem on my own, a comparison of conditioning when the shock was avoidable and when it was not. The behavior of the animals (goats) when

the shock could be avoided by raising the leg to which the electrode was attached was adaptive; the animals quickly learned to lift the leg and settled
down to an economical and uniform response. When the shock could not
be avoided, there were frequent shifts from one action to another, all of them
belonging to a natural escape and defense repertory, such as retreating backward, or rearing. The results supported a two-factor learning theory that
was popular at the time. I was happy to get back to studying learning, and
gave a report on the research at the next meeting of the Eastern Psychological
Association.

Goats were actually bred at the Behavior Farm, and a number of pairs of
them (always twins) were born every year in the late winter. It seemed to me
a wonderful opportunity to undertake a developmental study of this
precocial animal. I had never done developmental research, but it appealed
to me very much, especially when one had some control over rearing and
could make observations from birth onwards (I was vague about how long,
but at least until the animals were turned out with the herd and could be observed with them). One of every pair of twins could be treated experimen-
tally, while the other served as control. I was interested in the role of the
mother immediately following birth in relation to development of herd be-

Fig. 13. Eleanor Gibson
at the Behavior Farm, holding
a young kid, with Jerry and
Jean.

havior. I consequently attended the births (often on cold February nights) of eight pairs of twins, destined to be reared with their own mothers or foster mothers, a peer group, or alone (the latter two groups fed artificially from a nipple pail). Observations were made from birth at frequent intervals for evidence of possible imprinting and maternal–kid inter- actions of various kinds.

It became clear that the maternal goat, if deprived of her offspring for even a few hours after birth, did not welcome it and would even butt it rudely away if it came near her and tried to nurse. Licking the newborn kid and other chemical interchanges are important (as any farmer could no doubt have told me). The kid on the other hand would approach any adult female for days after birth. Imprinting did not occur very early, but it would eventually, perhaps to its peer group or even a human caretaker, if the kid were deprived of its mother.

An interesting observation came out of the early stages of this research (fortunately, as the research did not get very far). I was especially interested in chemical information as a factor in bonding, so at most of the births I removed the (experimental) kid from the mother before she could lick it and before the afterbirth appeared. The kid was immediately bathed in a detergent. On one occasion, I had just completed the first kid's bath when its twin began to make an appearance. What to do in a hurry with the freshly bathed one? The farm manager, watching from a half-door, said, "Put it on the stand." The stand was a very high camera stand with a pedestal about a foot square. I protested that it would fall off, but he assured me that it would not. I stood the damp little animal on the stand, and there it remained, upright, looking around the room, until I could carry it off to its assigned place. Goats are prepared from birth to survive on a precipice and this lesson was good preparation for the visual cliff experiment conducted a few years later.

My first essay into developmental research ceased not long afterward. I discovered on returning after Easter weekend that some of my carefully reared (so far) subjects had been given away as Easter presents. The farm manager assured me that this was customary, and anyhow, he said, he could tell me what would have happened. The experiment was ruined, and I left the Behavior Farm somewhat discouraged by my foray into a new field of research. It would be quite a while before I got back to the study of development, but I had discovered that I wanted to, and I would when I could acquire a lab of my own. Meanwhile, I needed a new research project and a new sponsor, hopefully a more reliable one. I had friends at the Perceptual and Motor Skills Laboratory at Lackland Air Force Base, which supported outside research. I negotiated a contract with them to study estimation of distance under natural outdoor conditions. This was to be a training study, so I would get back to my originally chosen field of learning again, albeit in the most different possible setting from my last learning study, conditioning the goats.

The contract came through, with three studies planned and enough money to pay me and a research assistant. There was one truly serendipitous arrangement. Sampson Air Force Base, which specialized in the induction of new trainees, was quite near Ithaca, and it was arranged that when our research was ready to go, a busload of new trainees would be sent over each day to serve as participants. We were delighted and the trainees, when they came, enjoyed it too. A sergeant came with them, to keep them in order, presumably.

We were interested in giving training that would generalize, so we had to plan a series of judgments that would all differ in ground features, permitting a large number of judgments of different ground stretches. Because we were working during the summer months, the university allowed us to use a very long athletic field (132 × 488 yards). By means of the strategy of changing station points for making the judgments (six different stations), we provided 108 different stretches of distance for judgment. Targets were constructed to yield no cues. Two groups of participants were run, a control group and an experimental group that was given correction during a training series. The participants made judgments of distance in yards. All took part in a pretest and a posttest, which were identical but differed from any of the distance stretches used for training. The training was effective in improving the accuracy of judgments, and the posttest judgments, although uncorrected, were more accurate than the pretest judgments, so there was presumably transfer. The experimental group was significantly more accurate, as might be expected, than the control group.

We were still dubious about the generalizability of the training, as participants were making the same type of judgments on the same field. Consequently, training in the next experiment was conducted in a different space (the quadrangle of the Arts College), and a different method of training was used. Participants divided up the space (350 yards long) into progressively smaller fractions. A moving marker was provided by a bicycle that cycled away from participants and kept moving until a participant judged that it had reached the correct division point and blew a whistle. A marker was placed at the correct point, with the number of yards distant painted on it, so that the participant was aware of errors and could construct a sort of mental scale. The bicycle rider, incidentally, attracted a great deal of attention from passersby and we always had an audience. Following the training period, the participants were driven to the same field used in the first experiment and given the same set of test judgments of distance in yards to 18 targets. Compared with a control group, whom they surpassed, preliminary training with a yard scale of distance did yield transfer to a new locale and unfamiliar targets. A second experiment, in which similar training was followed by relative judgments of distance, did not result in transfer, however. Whatever the participants were learning, it was not an increase in sensitivity. A further experiment on fractionation of distance (stretches of surface over the ground) established that individuals can make such judgments quite accurately, and that no improvement results from simple correction of errors.

I decided, after these experiments, that what the participants given training were learning was a conceptual scale to which perception of ground surfaces could be related. Sensitivity to small differences in surface stretches was not affected. Was this, then, a typical specimen of perceptual learning? Perceptual learning was the concept that I had decided would be the hub at which my varied ventures in research would be aimed. My husband and I discussed perceptual learning at length and devised an experiment together (a rare event) to clarify the concept and demonstrate its theoretical value. My husband was interested in perceptual learning because of his research on learning to identify aircraft during World War II. I had written my dissertation about the importance of "differentiation learning" of a set of drawn nonsense forms. From these two sources we came up with an experiment that we thought had to do with learning to perceive. We referred to it as "identification learning," a name that fitted the aircraft task and the drawn forms in my old experiment. Our hypothesis was that the learner had to narrow down a mass of stimulus information until only that which uniquely specified a particular item remained, a process of differentiation. This process might especially coincide with and characterize development.

We argued that there were two alternative theories of perceptual learning—the enrichment theory and the specificity theory. According to the former, perceptual learning is a matter of enriching (adding to) previously meager sensations, traditionally by some associative process. According to the second alternative, perception comes to be in better and better correspondence with the information in the environment, which in any given event becomes more distinctive. We wrote at that time that perceptual learning results in responding to variables of physical stimulation not previously responded to. What is perceived is thus differentiated from other potentially confusable items or events. The experiment that was to illustrate this view was run (by me) at Smith College, during my last year there when I was teaching a learning course. We reported it in 1950 at the meeting of the

American Psychological Association, but in the flurry of moving to Cornell, we didn't publish it until later.

In the experiment, we presented the participant with a single nonsense "scribble" to study, and then showed it mixed in with a set of 17 scribbles all varying from it in some systematic way. Items identical to the target item were shuffled in a pack of cards with the others and the participant was to identify the target item on each run through the pack, after it was shuffled. The participants did indeed confuse the items at first, and succeeded (with correction) in consistently identifying the target items. There were three groups of participants—adult colleagues, college students, and children. The children needed more trials, but all succeeded in differentiating the target item from the foil items. Although we left the experiment in a file while we settled down at Cornell, it saw the light again, as I shall tell shortly.

7

Visiting in Academe

We settled happily at Cornell. I continued to find opportunities for research and the children grew and made friends. As James expanded his research program, his book *Perception of the Visual World* was published, and he published papers with some very new ideas. His reputation grew. He was invited to the University of California at Berkeley as visiting professor. We decided to spend one semester there (first term of 1954–55), although it meant changing the children's schools. A nice house on Grizzly Peak (wonderful name) was found for us, and Jerry enrolled for his first year of high school at the Berkeley High School, large and reputed to have a population of "toughs." I think we didn't quite realize just how traumatic this experience might be for him! I had no job and no opportunity for research, but there were interesting people (Edward Tolman and Egon Brunswik among others), I wrote things up, and we made good friends. The American Association for the Advancement of Science (AAAS) had scheduled its annual Christmas meeting there, so James and Leo Postman, a colleague at Berkeley, planned a symposium on perceptual learning. The Gibsons were to present their theory (and my old scribble experiment) on "Perceptual Learning as Differentiation" and Postman was to reply, espousing "Enrichment Theory." A lively debate was held and the two papers published. The arguments were very good-natured and enjoyed by all.

Our paper (J. J. Gibson & E. J. Gibson, 1955a) described the scribble experiment that I had run earlier, and maintained that perceptual learning was a narrowing down, an increase in correspondence of perceived properties with physical properties and objects in the environment, becoming in greater and greater correspondence with stimulation, not less, as an enrichment or an add-on theory would maintain. We learn to perceive more qualities or features of things, and they become more distinctive. Our experiment bore this out, as even the youngest participants learned to identify the target drawing, confusion decreased, and they soon were able to point out the dimensions in which the items differed.

Postman's (1955) paper emphasized the associationism of present behavior theory and maintained that perceptual learning should be thought of in stimulus–response terms. He stressed that changes in response are part and parcel of the problem of perceptual learning and that accounting for these changes in response inevitably endows the problem of perceptual learning with an associative component. It was a good argument. He maintained that stimulus–response analysis was essential for understanding meaning, and that the organism has learned to perceive the meaning of a stimulus when it has learned the proper response. The specificity theory had no testable hypothesis to account for such changes, he insisted. In a sense, he was right, and we can do better by this time, as I intend to show later.

One outcome of our visit to Berkeley was an offer to James to join the faculty at Berkeley. We had indeed enjoyed our stay, but we did not feel permanently attracted to the place. They made no offer to me, either. Perhaps that would have made a difference, but neither did I see a clear opening for research there, and we returned to Cornell, happy to get home. Besides, Berkeley High School was really an intimidating place. The Ithaca High School was not so great, but at least not scary. We returned to the Berkeley area in September 1955, however, when James gave the Presidential Address for Division 3 (Experimental Psychology) of the American Psychological Association. It was a wonderful talk, incorporating our experiment on perspective transformations with a shadow caster, demonstrating their information for depth (J. J. Gibson & E. J. Gibson, 1957). He showed a film of the shadow caster display (always seen as an object moving in depth). The final display of the film was four layers of surface (actually made from wire net) all moving at once in different arcs, separated, with beautifully visible paths of motion. We made the film ourselves, our children helping, each of us moving (off screen) a wire surface in a practiced rotation. Constancy of shape, rigidity, and four paths of rotation (whose angle of arc can be estimated accurately) are all perceived at once, albeit from a flat screen. The audience was impressed, as they should have been.

Although we had not yet spent 6 years at Cornell, my husband had bargained (before coming) for credit for years at Smith, and so the following year he had a sabbatical leave. He had been offered a Fulbright Fellowship at Oxford University. A year abroad! We went. The college we were to be affiliated with was Magdalen. We did not know anyone there, but "the Professor" had his secretarial help find us a house, and we located schools for the children. Jerry's was a so-called "public" school, St. Edwards, in Oxford and he was expected to live there as a boarder. Jean was enrolled at the Headington School for girls. It was a boarding school, but with younger day pupils, and we considered her too young to board. We met another family with children, going to Oxford, the Smithies, on the ship traveling to England. That was a good thing, because we found that friends did not come so easily there as in our own country.

The house found for us was in Wheatley, a village outside Oxford. The house was old, dark, and from an American's point of view, dirty, inconvenient, and cold. There was a nice family in the village who had a daughter Jean's age. They kindly offered to drive Jean with her to school and back, but that was the only advantage. Our courage failed us, after a short try, and we looked for other quarters. We found an apartment, newly created, on the third floor of a very large old North Oxford house. It was the home of the Macbeth family (Mr. Macbeth was a professor of ophthalmology at Oxford, but as a surgeon, was always addressed as Mr.). The apartment was clean, light, fairly warm, and rather small, but attractive. We had to walk up through the Macbeths' living quarters to get to ours, but if they didn't mind, why should we? Besides, doors to rooms are always closed in England! The Macbeths had four children, Anne and Alistair, both through school; a younger girl, Katie, Jean's age; and a younger boy, Fergus. We all liked each other at once. We had only two bedrooms, one very small, but there was room for a cot for Jerry on the few occasions when he could stay with us in the very large, empty, third-floor hall. There was a convenient bus that Jean could take to school and a schoolmate lived next door, so we settled in with a feeling of relief.

We did not settle in so well at Magdalen College, however. Magdalen College did not have a modern laboratory building. I was given a small bare room in the old stone building that housed the psychologists, and my husband was given the largest room (once the parlor) in a house nearby. Neither boasted a desk, they were very cold, and hopeless for research. In any case, we had no equipment. The Professor was not interested in perception, and the only young Fellow who was, Stuart Sutherland, seemed suspicious of us and not very friendly. After a few rather futile efforts at setting up some makeshift arrangements in my cold cell, we decided to put our efforts into writing and making the most of our overseas location. Experimental research was better done in Ithaca, and the opportunities for finding out what psychologists in England and Europe were doing were more or less at our doorstep.

We began our visits to other laboratories during the Christmas vacation. We had purchased a small British Ford soon after our arrival in Oxford. It was essential during our short stay in Wheatley, and useful afterward for marketing, which had to be done daily. Besides, there were excursions to make. When the childrens' schools closed for Christmas vacation, we crossed the English Channel to Ostend and then proceeded to Louvain, Belgium, where we were to spend Christmas with our friends Pat and Olie Smith, also on leave for the year. The attraction at Louvain was Professor Albert Michotte, a baron and an ardent Catholic, as well as one of the great psychologists of perception. He welcomed us to his laboratory with great cordiality, and James found his ideas attractive, not at all in conflict with his own. Michotte was particularly interested in the perception of causality, and espoused the idea that perception could be "amodal"—a far cry from either sensation-based views of perception or the stimulus–response learning theory in vogue in the United States at the time.

We had a pleasant Christmas with the Smiths, and a few days later the two families set forth, the Gibsons in the little Ford and the Smiths in their new Volkswagen, for a voyage south. We went first to Paris, of course; then we drove all the way down the Rhone, and finally into Italy, having picnics and staying where it pleased us, in inexpensive hostelries. It was pure fun, a memorable trip. Unfortunately, I picked up a hepatitis virus somewhere on the way, but it did not make itself known until after we had reached our Oxford home again.

I was very ill with hepatitis, and spent several weeks in an Oxford nursing home. I did recover finally, but I accomplished little professionally that year. James, on the other hand, wrote what I consider his most interesting paper, one that foreshadowed ideas that he would develop for the rest of his life. The paper, "Visually Controlled Locomotion and Visual Orientation in Animals and Man" (J. J. Gibson, 1958), was published in the British Journal of Psychology (a gesture of thanks to Britain in a way). It was recently republished on its 40th anniversary by the Journal of Ecological Psychology, accompanied by a number of new papers on locomotion in the same tradition.

James gave talks at British universities, and we traveled again, come spring vacation, this time to Cornwall, another memorable trip. One result of our Oxford experience was a decision to send Jerry on our return to finish high school at Deerfield Academy. St. Edward's was not comfortably warm and the food was dismal, but it did dispense serious education. We decided that the Ithaca High School would not do. Jean joyously threw her school shoes ("sturdies") into the Atlantic on the sea voyage home, but her experience had been a good one. She even had a British accent for a short while.

Our other trips to European universities were made purely professionally and without the children. We traveled to Innsbruck, Austria, to visit Ivo Kohler (no relation to the Köhler of Gestalt psychology). Ivo Kohler had performed many experiments using distorting lenses and prisms of various kinds, studying the way people adapted to them and the after-effects they engendered. My husband had tried wearing wedge prisms briefly and had studied adaptation to curvature and its after-effects during our years at Smith. He had found, surprisingly, that there was adaptation to the curvature of a line, followed by a negative aftereffect (reverse curvature) even when the observer was not wearing a distorting instrument, if the line was stared at long enough. Ivo Kohler's work was notable because he or one of his students had worn various kinds of distorting instruments over very long periods of time while pursuing their daily lives. He found that under these circumstances, adaptation to the distorted information is related to ongoing actions. He called this change "conditional adaptation" followed by "situational after-effects." It seems that the nature of the perceptual aberration depended on the direction in which the wearer's vision deviated from straight ahead. Objectively vertical lines were displaced one way when seen from below and another when looked at from above, both happening in the same retinal area (see Kohler, 1964).

I tried to make this clear in my book on perceptual learning (E. J. Gibson, 1969). What is clear is that perception and action cannot be divorced, and that we are able to extract constant properties of the real world around us only by finding invariant properties over many changes. The world looks distorted when one first wears prisms, but after getting about and acting in it for a while, one perceives things as they are. Adaptation of this kind is an active process, not the same as James's finding of the straightening of a single curved line. Perception in that case did not gradually become more veridical, as it does with the long wearing of prisms (or with our own spectacles). It is interesting, though, that however distorted this world looks when one first puts on the prisms, there is complete transfer of the meanings of things. One may fall down the crooked-looking or out-of-line stairs while trying to descend them,

Fig.14. The Gibsons visiting Professor Ivo Kohler and colleague
at the University of Innsbruck.

but it is perfectly clear that they are stairs and what we are supposed to use them for. That is perceptual learning, too, and it is lasting.

In the following years, often on the occasion of an iternational congress, we visited other European psychologists. The most important of these visits (which happened more than once) was to Professor Gunnar Johansson at the University of Uppsala in Sweden. The Johanssons visited us in Ithaca, too, becoming our close friends. Johansson was particularly interested in the perception of motion in events; his monograph *Configurations in Event Perception* (Johansson, 1950) was published the same year as *The Perception of the Visual World* (J. J. Gibson, 1950) and James and Johansson had much in common. Both were impressed with the role of motion in stimulus information and the part it played in depth perception. Both were convinced that what we perceive are events. Perception necessarily continues over time, as invariant information about the world is extracted. Many years later, in 1976 following the International Congress of Psychology in Brussels, we visited in Uppsala, and stayed at the Johansson's summer home on the Baltic Sea as well. James was presented with an Honorary Doctor of Science degree by Uppsala University. This was an extraordinary occasion by American standards. He wore a coronet of laurel leaves on his head in the procession of dignitaries!

Another university that we visited more than once was the University of Edinburgh. The Professor there was James Drever, whom we had met earlier. There was also David Lee, a student and eventually longtime friend of ours, an exceedingly clever and productive experimenter. On one visit to the University of Edinburgh, that university also awarded James an honorary degree.

In 1966 there was an International Congress of Psychology in Moscow. An unlikely time, it might seem, because Russia was a communist country and there was a cold war on. But Russian psychology was flourishing. There was Vygotsky, an internationally known psychologist, and other Russian psychologists who were keenly interested in perceptual learning and had a theory of it (a motor theory, of course, though not specifically Pavlovian). There was to be a symposium on perceptual learning and I was invited to give one of the papers. So was Richard Held, another American psychologist; Éliane Vurpillot, a French psychologist with whom I was acquainted; and several Russians, including Zaporozhets, Zinchenko, and Julia Gippenreiter. The symposium went well and the papers were all published in the proceedings. The Congress was well attended and peaceful, marked for us by one memorable occasion.

Fig. 15. James Gibson (far left) after receiving an honorary degree at the University of Uppsala in 1976. Note his crown of laurels.
(From left to right are James Gibson, Karin Runeson receiving her PhD, Gunnar Johansson, and Eleanor Gibson.)

The occasion was a dinner party held by Professor Zaporozhets for the members of his symposium in his own private apartment (very small by American standards). It was a sit-down dinner, prepared by his wife. The food was good, the wine flowed, and cheery toasts were made. I have a vivid mental picture of Richard Held getting up, raising his glass, and urging heartily, "May all our two countries' meetings be as happy as this one." Alas, I have never seen our Russian colleagues again, although our hope at that time was very high that every congress would renew our acquaintance.

A few years later we visited Fabio Metelli, an Italian perception psychologist at the University of Padua. He had arranged a tour of Italian universities for us, prepared the itinerary, readied our host at each one, and got the whole trip paid for by NATO. The latter feature made my husband very uneasy, and the tour actually was not as pleasant as it may sound. We didn't know most of our hosts, few of them seemed to be at all interested in perception, and we had no audience for talks because the students were striking all over Italy and in most cases had succeeded in closing the universities. It turned out to be a sightseeing trip, winding up in Sicily. We visited both Catania and Palermo. We wondered rather uneasily if our hosts, although both major university professors, might be members of the mafia. We never saw one of them, but his son conducted our sightseeing tour, taking us up Mt. Etna, among other tourist attractions. Academically, it was not a successful visit. It did not include the University of Trieste, which had (and has) a fine reputation in psychology. But doubtless there was a strike there, too! We weren't sorry to get back to work.

8

Midlife Without Crises

Midlife is often considered a risky time, not to be celebrated as one's best years. But I believe this period has been much maligned. You've figured out what you want to do; you have your health and strength, a home and some friends. Best of all, it seems to me a very productive time. It was for us. We had a home we loved, good friends, good students, and work that we could hardly wait to do. Our two children were handsome, smart, and charming. Furthermore, they went away to prep school. The Ithaca High School was not too good, so the fall following our return from Oxford, Jerry went off to Deerfield Academy, near our old home in Northampton. We knew of it (only good things) from friends at Smith who had sent their sons there. Deerfield was very generous to us financially, too. Jean was still at home for a while, and then she went off to Northfield School for Girls, also in Massachusetts. The Northfield girls had to do a little housework, as well as study, and that was just fine. Both schools were a great success. And what were the parents doing, meanwhile? We were working.

And were there really no crises? Yes, I suppose there were, but they must have been minor, because they're impossible to remember now. James and I argued (noisily, according to our children) quite often, but not about domestic affairs; we argued about ideas. That was not because we had no respect for each other's views, either; far from it. Perhaps it was because with no teaching position, only off-and-on projects, I needed a vent. But I think it was because we respected each other's views and were both very interested in the problems we discussed. It was usually profitable intellectually. I know my husband thought that I was a good experimenter, and I thought he was the greatest psychologist of the century (and I still do). What were we thinking about and working on that inspired so much discussion?

Somewhere along the way during our year at Oxford, we visited Piaget's laboratory in Geneva. I have very little memory of it either then or on later occasions when I visited there. But I was still interested in development, despite the fiasco of my first attempt at a rearing experiment with the newborn goats. The following years working on perception of distance and depth were satisfying, and I knew the time was well spent, but I needed to get back to my own niche, as I began to think of it. I had been particularly impressed by the experiment of Lashley and Russell (1934) with rats leaping from a jumping stand to a landing platform. Rats reared in darkness took no longer to learn to gauge the distance than rats reared in the light. Lashley's student, Hebb, was achieving fame for his rearing experiments (Hebb, 1937) and for his neurophysiological developmental theory. This area of research attracted me. I had a new colleague, Richard Walk, who taught courses on learning in the Cornell Psychology Department and had a rat lab. Walk and I agreed to collaborate on some early rearing experiments with rats and we were awarded a grant by the National Science Foundation. We began with an experiment rearing infant rats in an "enriched" environment (E. J. Gibson & Walk, 1956). Infant hooded rats were exposed from birth to cut-out metal shapes (triangles and circles) hung on their cage walls, and then at 3 months of age were compared with control rats (reared without shapes) in an experiment in which they had to discriminate these shapes from one another. The experiment worked at first, but repetitions and further experiments made it seem unlikely that the rats needed to learn to see these figures as discrete shapes. In a later experiment, rats reared in the dark (E. J. Gibson, Walk, & Tighe, 1959) learned to discriminate them as easily as did the light-reared control animals. After a series of studies of passive enhancement and deprivation with rats, it began to be clear that a theory of perceptual development should not be based on passive exposure to features of the environment in early development. Mere exposure to curvature, angles, and so on was not the stuff of perceptual development, although a popular theory of the time would have it so.

Our rather negative conclusions about the value of augmenting or depriving early environments of formal architectural features rewarded us, fortunately, with one serendipitous outcome. Rearing rats in the dark was a very troublesome chore. We decided, before removing a final group of them to the light at 3 months of age, that we would make our work pay doubly by giving them another test immediately upon moving them into the light. It was to be a test of depth perception. Of course, there was already Lashley's experiment with the jumping stand, but it required days of training. We would avoid the training period by simply placing them next to a cliff and watching to see if they walked off. They were to be protected from falling by clear glass, lighted from below, placed over the void. Our research assistant, Thomas Tighe, and I hurriedly put together a contraption made from material we could find around the lab—a large sheet of glass, mounted with clamps, on some upright metal standards. Under half of the glass we placed a patterned surface (some checked wallpaper); about 4 feet below the other side was the same wallpaper on the floor. We put a narrow strip of wood across the middle where the rat would be placed at the start. It would jump off, we thought, but which way? To the safe-looking ground or to the apparent deep drop-off on the other side?

Half our rats had been reared in the light as a control group. Litters of infant rats had been split, soon after birth, before their eyes opened, so the light- and dark-reared groups were siblings, so to speak. At 90 days of age, the rats (the light-reared first) were placed on our makeshift "cliff." All the animals, after a swift glance around, descended to what we dubbed the "shallow" side, and walked about until they were replaced in their cages. Although a few climbed back onto the strip of wood, they did not venture onto the "deep" side. Now what would their dark-reared brethren do? We watched in fascination as every one of them repeated the behavior of the light-reared animals.

Impressed as we were, we worried. Could it be that one side of the room was more attractive—warmer, darker, more odiferous? We thought of a control condition, and placed the patterned wallpaper on both sides of the apparatus, so both were equally shallow. All the rats were given a second run. This time they descended willy-nilly, to one side or the other, and then wandered back and forth. Tom watched with eyes popping, and then said, unforgettably, "I'd never have believed it if I hadn't seen it." So, the cliff worked, and we concluded that hooded rats were capable of discriminating depth and avoiding a cliff even when deprived of all light during the first 90 days of development (Walk, Gibson, & Tighe, 1957).

We proceeded to build a more adequate cliff apparatus and planned a number of comparative experiments, including two with newborn animals capable of locomotion at birth. These were baby chicks and kids (baby goats) less than a day old. These precocial animals, 100% of them, avoided the cliff side of the apparatus at once, showing as clear evidence of discrimination as any adult animal. I was not surprised at the behavior of the kids, having witnessed the "real thing," so to speak, in my days at the Behavior Farm. However, kittens reared in the dark, brought out and tested when their eyes had opened, did not follow the pattern of the dark-reared rats. They wandered about on either side of our enlarged apparatus, and even bumped into the side wall. They needed experience with visually guided steering of locomotion, it appeared. They did not need to fall off anything, or to be taught the dangers of a drop-off, however. After bringing them into the light, we put them on the cliff apparatus again each day for several days. After 2 days in the light, 80% of them avoided the deep side, and after 6 days they all did. Experience should have taught them that the deep side was as safe as the shallow, if avoidance of a cliff depended on tuition about safety or on fear induced by falling.

Of course, we proceeded to build a cliff for observing human infants. It was my first experience experimenting with them. How did one get participants? We put an ad in the newspaper, asking for crawling babies, offering them $3.00 for taking part in an experiment. My husband said, "You won't get anyone. They'll think you're going to shock the babies." I had shocked goats and sheep, after all! But the telephone in the lab rang and rang, and people brought us crawling babies. They ranged widely in age (6 ½ –12 months). Most of them avoided the deep side, even when their mothers entreated them to cross it. We concluded that perception of depth has developed by the time locomotion is possible in human infants. That is undoubtedly true, we now know. However, it is also true that crawling experience makes a difference for navigation. Brand new crawlers are apt to descend to the deep side of the cliff as often as to the shallow. It's not because they can't perceive depth, but because they require some experience in visually guiding locomotion before reliable selection of surfaces develops. They learn which surfaces afford safe locomotion by crawling about in their own homes. Only considerable later research (mostly done by other experimenters) revealed this fact. But the babies on the cliff were well publicized by an article in the *Scientific American* (E. J. Gibson & Walk, 1960), and we had achieved fame of sorts.

My research with Walk continued until the fall of 1959 when James and I went off to spend a year at the Institute for Advanced Study in Princeton. At the end of that year Walk left Cornell, moving to George Washington University. That meant that I no longer had a laboratory to work in, so I did no further research with the cliff. However, I was hooked on developmental studies by that time, and I knew where I was heading. A new op-

Fig. 16. The visual cliff: Infant approaching on shallow side and hesitating at deep side. (From E. J. Gibson and R. D. Walk, The Visual Cliff, Scientific American, 1960, 202, p. 165).

portunity to work with children arose, and I embarked on a problem that was entirely new to me—how does one learn to read? More about that later.

During this time, James's research on perception was flourishing. He had many excellent graduate students, his seminar was a weekly source of excitement, and his theory of perception became even more radical, as the old guard saw it. The 1950 book, *Perception of the Visual World*, was hailed as a great success, but he felt more and more that it did not go far enough in discarding the old idea that perception was constructed from sensations. He worked on a new book, in which he would introduce the idea that perception is "direct," not a composition of prior sensations; that it is unified, and motivated by a very active search for information. His ideas did not leave the perceiver "buried in thought," because he considered that perceiving was part of behavior, and that a perceptual system included active mechanisms of adjustment (e.g., pointing the eyes to focus on something, turning the head to hear, moving the fingers over an object to feel), and moreover the direction of action. He introduced such terms as *ordinal stimulus* and *higher order relations* to show that information obtained from stimulation might be in direct correspondence with what is perceived.

As I mentioned earlier, he formed a habit, not long after coming to Cornell, of writing a page or two on the topic for discussion in his upcoming weekly seminar. These short essays were duplicated by a ditto process that turned out copies in purple ink. They were always provocative and they did indeed stimulate excited discussions. They were dubbed, appropriately, "purple perils." A large number of them have been assembled and copied (Pittenger, Reed, Kim & Best, 1997) and are now available on the Internet. I include a paragraph from one written in 1954 to give the flavor of my husband's thinking at that time.

> One more example of an ordinal stimulus must suffice—this one only to show that novel hypotheses can be generated by the theory. What is the relation between concomitant or simultaneous stimuli from different modalities of sense? The stability and constancy of visual perception probably depends in large part on such a relation. Consider the rotation of the retinal image which occurs when a man tilts his head to one side and the fact that his phenomenal world nevertheless remains upright. The significant fact may be the vestibular and kinesthetic stimulation which accompanies the retinal stimulation and which enters into the whole as a component. When two component changes vary reciprocally an invariant product exists. Can such an invariant itself be considered a stimulus? If so the constant uprightness of the visual world is a matter of correspondence with the stimulus, not a lack of correspondence. The relevant stimulus is only more complex than we had realized.

The topic of multidimensional perception thus introduced here was very new and led eventually to a great many experiments. Dozens of new concepts were introduced, and terminology gradually changed with them. As I leaf through the collected purple perils, I am struck by how familiar now what was remarkably novel then often appears. Consider, for example, a short essay on "What Is Perceived? Notes for a Reclassification of the Visible Properties of the Environment." There are three major headings, "Spatial Properties", "Spatiotemporal Properties" and "The Visual Detection of the Self." How remarkably modern the third one sounds! Spatial properties included surface layout, substance or composition, and lighting or illumination. Spatiotemporal properties included "motions of rigid objects," "deformations of elastic objects," "progressive occlusion and disocclusion," the "ending and beginning of the solid state," the "onset and cessation of illumination," "animate motions and deformation," and "events in general." This list provided a program for research, and research there was, despite the crowded quarters in Morrill Hall. Graduate students who worked with James included Walter Carel, Janet Cornsweet, Fred Dibble, Dickens Waddell, Jacob Beck, Jean Purdy, Lois Lawrence, Alfred Steinschneider, Richard Bergman, John Hay, Howard Flock, Anne and Herb Pick, William Schiff, James Caviness, Fred Backlund, George Kaplan, Horace Reynolds, Kirk Wheeler, Philip Kaushall, Anthony Barrand, and others who visited, sometimes from abroad. I am afraid I have forgotten some of the names, alas.

Finding room for students, research, and visitors became such a problem that Cornell, sometime during the 1960s, presented us with new quarters (new to us, that is). The place was a building at the Ithaca airport that had been built for some project of General Electric (GE). GE moved to a new, much grander building and we inherited the old one. It was light and roomy, and no one cared if walls were knocked down or odd experimental spaces were created. No members of the Psychology Department except the Gibsons and their students moved out there, but a secretary was provided and there was plenty of room for everyone, including myself! There was a big seminar room, ample office space, good research space and easy parking (but of course one had to drive out from campus). Getting participants there for experiments was not quite so easy. But on the whole, it worked well and became a little world of psychologists on its own. Many papers were written, many discussions were held, and many experiments were set up. Many guests from other universities at home and from abroad came—Gunnar Johansson, Fred and Ulla Backlund and Gunnar Jansson from Sweden, Kai vonFieandt from Finland, and David Lee from Edinburgh, all of whom spent a semester or longer with us. Many others came for shorter periods.

All through this period, James's research and his seminar were flourishing and new ideas were being noted every week in the purple perils. But getting it all together in an orderly flow in a book was another matter. There simply wasn't time for such an extended work. He was determined, however, to make it clear in print that perception was not based on a retinal image but on information in the light, that perceptual systems were actively seeking information, that perception directly picked up invariants over time, and other equally radical ideas. The opportunity to work on this project came in 1958–59 when he received a grant from the National Science Foundation to spend the year at the Institute for Advanced Study at Princeton. Of course I went along. Our children were away at school now, Jean at the Northfield School for Girls and Jerry beginning college at Harvard, so we were free to spend the year away from Ithaca. My self-assigned task, along with writing up research and meeting papers, was to think about perceptual learning, now the focus of my work, and how it was related to development.

The Institute for Advanced Study at Princeton is home to many "hard" scientists and mathematicians, as well as scholars concerned with the humanities. However, there were few, if any, psychologists as colleagues. That did not really matter to us, because we had old friends in the Psychology Department at Princeton University. Two of James's old professors, H. S. Langfeldt and Leonard Carmichael, though retired, were still present, and his old classmate and graduate school companion Charles Bray was on the faculty. Katie Bray, his wife, was a Smith graduate, as I was. When we felt like socializing, there was good company at hand. The Princeton department was in need of new blood at the time, and while we were there, James was urged to join that department. However, our loyalties were by then with Cornell. I doubt, too, that I would have been offered even research opportunities at an all-male university, as Princeton was.

James made progress on his book, but slowly. I made little progress on a book, except that I thought about my problem and got my ideas clearer. During the year I was offered a welcome opportunity, however. Two Cornell professors, Harry Levin and Alfred Baldwin, both from the Department of Human Development, approached me and urged me to join them in an about-to be-formed interdisciplinary consortium devoted to basic research on the reading process. The researchers were to include developmental and experimental psychologists and linguists. It was to be fully funded by federal agencies and would have "relevance" as well as sound scholarly procedures. They needed an experimental psychologist and I was invited to be the one. I protested that I had only recently resolved to devote my best efforts to the topic of perceptual learning. They argued that the new enterprise would offer me opportunities to do this, and I was eventually persuaded that it would, as I contemplated possible experiments with children in the early stages of learning to read. It was a good moment to receive a new research offer, as it came just after I had discovered that Richard Walk would be leaving Cornell, ending my opportunity to work in his laboratory. The new program, called "Project Literacy" would have generous funds for graduate assistants and for me, a research associate. The airport laboratory would have room for us, and we might work in schools, too. My research was to be strictly experimental, however, on what was learned (and how) as reading skill is acquired. It had been many years since reading was a legitimate topic in experimental psychology—Woodworth's chapter in his classic *Experimental Psychology* (1938) having been the final contribution. The topic had been left to educators who were chiefly interested in questions of curriculum. Good

research had been performed early in the century by such respected psychologists as Cattell and Dodge. As psychology grew in importance as a science, however, reading as a topic fell into disrepute, although underlying
theoretical questions, such as the relation between speech and reading, remained unresolved. So I decided, eventually, to join the consortium and
gained many new friends and colleagues, as I tell later. I worked on reading
for nearly 12 years.

The year at Princeton came to an end with no new books finished. But we
were fortunate again; a few years later, in 1963–64, we were offered the opportunity to spend the year at the Center for Advanced Study in the Behavioral Sciences in Palo Alto, California. I was invited as a member of a
"cutting-edge" group that also included Lee Cronbach, Richard Atkinson,
and Jack Wohlwill. We were supposed to be making plans for educational
research, dear to the heart of Ralph Tyler, at that time director of the Center.
We did hold a conference supported by the Social Science Research Coun-
cil, and I wrote my first general paper about the reading process for it. But I
was able to spend a lot of my time thinking about, outlining, and beginning to
write the book I wanted to do on perceptual learning. James was able to go,
because the National Institutes of Health (NIH) had granted Cornell one of
their career research awards on his behalf. That meant he was excused from
routine teaching duties, and he spent a happy and very profitable year com-
pleting his book (actually rewriting most of it).

The new book, called *The Senses Considered as Perceptual Systems*, finally
appeared in print in 1966 (J. J. Gibson, 1966). It was, indeed, about perceptual systems, and the old doctrine that sensations were the basis of perception was jettisoned. As he put it,

> We shall have to conceive the external senses in a new way, as active rather
> than passive, as systems rather than channels, and as interrelated rather than
> mutually exclusive. If they function to pick up information, not simply to
> arouse sensations, this function should be denoted by a different term. They
> will here be called perceptual systems. (p. 47)

These systems are truly active, involving real movements. Movements are
of two kinds, exploratory and performatory, the first serving perception.
The search for information is an actual search, involving, for example, head
and eye movements in visual search, or fingering, rubbing, and prodding by
the haptic system.

Boring, the arch-psychophysicist of the century, when he first glanced at a
copy, wrote to James: "And then I got into the book and it takes only about
three minutes to see that this is quite a delightful book, a clear book, and it is as

much of a paradigm of good, biologically informed functional psychology as your other book was of perceptual phenomenology." From Boring that was high praise indeed. Of course, James had no sooner sent the book off to the publisher than he began to push his ideas about perception further, no longer seeing it as a matter of correspondence with stimulation, but as a search for relations between events and things in the world and the perceiver. But the ideas in this book had to come first, before the others could be entertained. Now I want to tell something about my own book, but that is another chapter.

9

The Decade of the Books

Wе returned to Cornell, with work and students ready to go. There was great pleasure in this homecoming. We had several times remodeled our house, extending the living room at one end and the kitchen at the other. We had a wonderful yard and good neighbors. James dropped into his favorite chair in his study and began writing again, which he always did far into the night. He was especially happy in his study and reveled in these solitary hours of thinking and writing. That was partly simply his nature, but there was a second reason. He was growing profoundly deaf, a condition inherited from his mother. He used a hearing aid, of course, but they were clumsy in those days and had to be stowed somewhere in one's clothing. The batteries always gave out at crucial times. His seminar did not suffer from this, because his graduate students were of course aware of the problem and always accommodated themselves and their speech to it; it was well worth it to them. Long sessions of communicating with students was exhausting, however, and he truly valued those hours after dinner, which became more and more extended. Fortunately, his disposition was naturally social and he never became a recluse.

I did a little shifting around in Jerry's room, now rarely inhabited, and made myself a fine place to write. There was a long shelf, table height, all across the far end, which he had used (I regret to say) for cleaning a hunting rifle. There was room for file cabinets under it, windows above it over-looked the backyard, and there were built-in bookshelves at one side. I took it over and began working on my book on perceptual learning at once. Time to write that book! I think of the period between 1969 and 1979 as the "decade of the books," because between us my husband and I pub-lished four books, this time two of them mine. My book *Principles of Percep-tual Learning and Development* appeared at last in 1969 (E. J. Gibson, 1969), only after many years of my working in the lab on related projects and contemplating a theory.

I had indeed been thinking about a theory of perceptual learning for a long time, and some of my research projects had turned me toward devel-opment, too. My ideas expanded enormously as I sat quietly in my little work room and considered all the topics I wanted to cover. I had a theory, of course, but I wanted one more fully developed than our earlier offering about differentiation as the major descriptive characterization (not that that wasn't right, and still is!). I also wanted the relevant facts, insofar as I could find research worthy of reporting. All the important kinds of behavior where perceptual learning occurs should be represented, if only to demon-strate how widespread and pervasive a process it is. I finally settled on 20 chapters, a long book. The first eight chapters were historical and also pre-sented my own theory.

I still called my theory a "differentiation" theory of perceptual learning, of course. It began with a discussion of generalization (I distinguished be-tween primary and secondary), discussed what is learned, emphasizing distinctive features and the increase in perceived specificity of the informa-tion that was used, and I gave many examples, some drawn from my ongo-ing research on learning to read. Achievement of specificity is facilitated when contrasting properties exist and are enhanced in the material to be differentiated. Critical properties must be extracted from the mass and ex-traneous or inconsistent ones filtered out. The process is an active one, a perceptual search for critical information. How is this search terminated? I thought by selective processes; not external rewards or punishment (al-though this idea was favored by several of my contemporaries), because perceptual learning, to my way of thinking, is a spontaneous self-motivated search for information, beginning in infancy and generally not open to the guidance of a teacher or intervention by an outsider. Correction by an out-sider would be tricky—how would such a person know what the learner was perceiving? What then can the selective factor be that brings about a narrowing down to the minimal critical information? I came up with a principle, the reduction of uncertainty:

> Consider in relation to this concept what is learned: distinctive features, invariants, and structure. They are the epitome of the reduction of uncertainty. Out of a mass of stimulus properties emanating from a set of objects, the perceiving organism learns to choose only those necessary for distinguishing between the objects. (E. J. Gibson, 1969, p. 140)

I gave examples of distinctive features learned (e.g., the aircraft recognition experiments), of invariants (learning to steer out of the way of a car veering toward you), and of structure (finding the order in all the arrays of things in the world, from human faces to heavenly bodies). One of my graduate students, Albert Yonas, performed an experiment designed to illustrate the process (Yonas & Gibson, 1967). I tried to show how "feedback loops" kept bringing new information to the learner to help the selective process.

There followed then four chapters on research areas that I considered highly relevant for perceptual learning, with summaries of the important research. They were "The Improvement of Perceptual Skills With Practice," "Perceptual Learning With Imposed Transformation of the Stimulus Array," "Intermodal Transfer of Perceptual Learning," and "The Study of Perceptual Development by Means of Controlled Rearing."

I interrupt my overview of the book here to give a little detail about one of these chapters. It deals with a topic that was "hot" for research at the time, produced some very interesting findings, and illustrated the broad applicability of my own theory to the field of perceptual learning. The chapter "Perceptual Learning With Imposed Transformation of the Stimulus Array" included experiments on wearing displacing prisms, fitted as spectacles over the eyes, which were very popular at the time. I had taken part myself in a minor experiment of this kind under my husband's direction as a student, and he was very familiar with the methods and the literature. We had actually traveled one summer, in 1956 at the end of our stay in Oxford, to the University of Innsbruck to visit Ivo Kohler, a professor there and the moving genius in the field of prism research (Kohler, 1964). Some of his more remarkable results were replicated by Herbert Pick and John Hay (1966) in experiments stretching over several summers at Cornell University. Indeed my daughter at the age of 18 took part as a participant one summer (well paid, of course), wearing distorting prisms constantly for 4 weeks. I cannot resist including a sonnet she wrote at the end of the time to commemorate the experience:

The World Thru 20-Diopter Prisms, Base Left
(After Wearing Them for Four Weeks)

The tipping floor and leering wall glare
And grasp, in league, Aggressive stairs approach
And pounce, looming chairs reach out to tear,
All stretches, shrinks, and flaming stains encroach.

With cunning steps I foil the league, with skill
The stairs subdue. From bolder feet the chairs retreat.
With steady view the stretchy rubbers still,
My confident gaze the glowing colors greet.

The bulges tease, the urchin dips appeal.
Two circling frames this fetching world enclose.
A euphoric cosmos the twin black frogs reveal.
The glowing world weighs gaily on my nose.

So vision is blurred, distorted, teased, reformed.
Can all the trusted standards be transformed?

Jean Gibson

One of the remarkable findings of these experiments was *conditional adaptation* (Kohler's term), renamed "gaze contingent adaptation" (Pick & Hay, 1966; Hay & Pick, 1966). For days Kohler had worn binocular half-prisms, causing his upward regard to pass through a 10° prism, while his downward regard passed through merely clear glass. His vision adapted differentially, depending on the direction of his regard; the same situation and objects gave rise to specific aftereffects with one line of regard, but not with the other. The effects were especially apparent in visual orientation and perceived movement. Pick and Hay replicated these observations and even found interocular transfer of the adaptation. It seemed to me that what the participant had done was to extract an intermodal, conditional invariant, learning to differentiate some very specific intermodal conditions, a process properly termed perceptual learning.

The next two chapters dealt with phylogenesis and comparative psychology, one of them devoted to imprinting (a stylish topic at the time, interesting to me because of my experiences at the Behavior Farm). The final six chapters of the book were concerned with ontogenetic development—a field that I now know to be of the very greatest importance for perceptual learning. However, the research to be drawn on at that time was meager, compared to the present wealth, and the methods for studying perceptual development in infants, though existing (preference and habituation were in use, and operant conditioning of infants was just being introduced), were still unsophisticated by present standards. Attention to the human face was a big topic, as it should have been. The research of Tom Bower, an old student of mine, stressed the early presence of object constancies (Bower, 1965, 1966), but was met by some with skepticism. Studies of development of surface perception and the layout of things were only beginning. I had a section on events, including the topic of object permanence (a few experiments with occlusion), enough to whet the appetite. Pictorial perception and of course language had chapters. The latter chapter appears (to me) more out of date than any of the rest of the book, the study of language perception having eclipsed by now the little we knew then. I wound up, in my last chapter, with "three trends in perceptual development" which I called (a) increasing specificity of discrimination, (b) the optimization of attention, and (c) increasing economy of information pickup and the search for invariance. These still sound right to me and I am proud of having expounded and stressed them.

Although this book took a long time in the writing, it was a real success, and I now believe I carved out a field for perceptual learning. As for perceptual development, it may have given a spur to the field. I hope so. Its day was dawning and I am astonished now as I contemplate the speed with which research has accumulated and how much it has contributed to our knowledge and theoretical sophistication. I was thrilled to receive the Century Award (given by the publisher, Appleton-Century-Crofts) for my book in 1969. Ulric Neisser, my colleague, had won it in 1966 for his book *Cognitive Psychology*. For Christmas following the award, I was sent a gorgeous leather-bound copy of the book, with inscriptions by all the psychology editors. One wrote, "My gratitude for a real winner." I felt proud. Not all the forthcoming criticism was wholly positive, however. A review in *Science*, titled "Processing Sensory Information," written by a chief information processor of the time, was dubious about including development and wrote:

It is essentially impossible to find out how a child or an animal knows the world; but it is quite easy (relatively speaking) to find out whether an organism can discriminate aspects of the world, and the discrimination procedures are the ones in use—with adults, capable of accepting complex instructions and of giving verifiable complex responses, we can learn much more about the nature of knowing, about perception as cognition. (Garner, 1970, p. 959)

Nonetheless, 10 years later, this book was named a "citation classic" (Current Contents, 1979), and I was asked to respond with why that should be. I think it was because it provided a framework for an important body of knowledge—what could be more important than the way we come prepared to learn to perceive the world and how we do it? I commented on this in my book *Odyssey* (E. J. Gibson, 1991) much later.

While I was engaged in writing this book, my status changed almost overnight. I mentioned that my husband was the recipient of a Senior Research Fellowship from NIH that actually paid his salary to the university until his retirement. That meant, because he was no longer on Cornell's payroll, that hiring his wife would no longer constitute nepotism. When this circumstance was fully realized, the department pushed for faculty status for me, and in 1966 after 16 years as research associate, I became a professor of psychology! Not assistant professor or associate professor, but the real thing, skipping all the boring and agonizing years of waiting for tenure. I had received enough recognition, it appeared, to warrant it (e.g., election to the Society of Experimental Psychologists). So 1966 was a great year, with the publication of James's book on the senses as perceptual systems (J. J. Gibson, 1966) and a professorship for me at last. It was a good thing, because my graduate students multiplied as I worked on the reading project, and I could now sign their documents myself.

The reading project turned out to be far more interesting than I had expected, and it broadened my life considerably. I made good friends with psychologists in the Department of Human Development—Harry Levin especially, but also Alfred Baldwin, Henry Ricciuti, George Suci, and John Condry. I had a number of wonderful graduate assistants, among them Anne Pick, Harry Osser, Albert Yonas, Carol Bishop, Nancy Rader, Richard Rosinski, and Yvette Tenney. I also made friends with faculty in the Department of Linguistics, including Charles Hockett, a nationally known linguist and one of the project members.

I started my new research with an experiment on how children learn to differentiate written symbols (E. J. Gibson, J. J. Gibson, Pick & Osser, 1962), a topic that fit well with my prior attempts to theorize about perceptual learning and so felt like familiar territory. Meanwhile, I was considering the question of how sound maps to letters, and vice versa. What determines the units for this two-way code, if one could call it a code? Certainly in English, one letter does not map neatly to one sound. Larger units would be more economical, in any case, but perhaps not practical for a starter. A transfer experiment showed me that knowledge of component relations facilitates transfer to reading new words. As a result I spent a lot of time investigating the spelling patterns of English, looking for rules and "higher order" units (which there are). As I put it in an article in *Science* in 1965:

> It is my belief that the smallest component units in written English are spelling patterns. By a spelling pattern I mean a cluster of graphemes in a given environment which has an invariant pronunciation according to the rules of English. These rules are the regularities which appear when, for instance, any vowel or consonant or cluster is shown to correspond with a given pronunciation in an initial, medial, or final position in the spelling of a word. (E. J. Gibson, 1965, p. 1068)

It will be noted that this idea fit in nicely with the Gibsonian concept of higher order invariants. It was also favored by at least one of the linguists (Charles Hockett) in our research consortium. We performed several experiments showing that pseudo-words containing legal spelling patterns were read with greater speed and accuracy than appropriate controls, such as the same letters printed in backward order.

Despite the fact that I was attracted, for a while, to an information-processing approach to reading, performing experiments on visual search, and obtaining confusion matrices to determine underlying distinctive features of letters, I was dissatisfied with the approach. Structural units, distinctive features, and a "decoding" approach are not sufficient for describing what a reader is doing. Perceptually speaking, reading is comparable to everyday perception of the world: It is a search for information that affords something for the perceiver. It is a truism (but worth repeating) that reading is a search for meaning. On the way to this conclusion, I wrote:

> Motivation and reinforcement for cognitive learning such as speech and reading are internal. Reinforcement is not reduction of a drive, but reduction of uncertainty, specifically the discovery of structure that reduces the information processing and increases cognitive economy. This is perceptual learning, not remembering something. (E. J. Gibson, 1970b, p.139)

Later on, I emphasized more strongly the function of reading, that it is a search for what the text affords, its value for the reader. Discovering order and rules enables the reader to extract larger semantic "chunks" as the task proceeds, so discovery of structure is important in learning to read, but the real task is to get the meaning, whatever the skill of the reader.

After nearly a decade of research on reading, I set out with my colleague Harry Levin to write a book about reading. We planned the chapters and divided them between us for writing the first drafts, but went over everything together. I took off a year, 1972–73, had my first and only sabbatical leave, and won a Guggenheim Fellowship. Harry was able to take the second semester away, too, so we left Ithaca to finish our work in Cambridge, Massachusetts. MIT generously offered us offices and secretarial help, and found a marvelous apartment for James and me at One Memorial Drive. The apartment looked out on the Charles River and we had the pleasure of watching the crews row up and down the river come spring. The chairman of the Psychology Department at that time was Hans Lucas Teuber, a genial scholar. We had other friends there, too, Richard Held in particular. There were still other friends at Harvard, so it was an enjoyable as well as a productive term.

The book was divided into three major sections. Part I we called "Concepts Underlying the Study of Reading." Four of the seven chapters were devoted to psychological concepts (including a theory of perceptual learning, of course), two to linguistic concepts and language development in children, and one to writing systems (including orthographic rules of English). Part II was called "The Study of Reading," with heavy emphasis on learning to read, and a discussion of learning from reading. One chapter was on models of the reading process, but we did not offer a model of our own, or espouse any other, because we thought of reading as being a highly functional, adaptive, and flexible process. A major reviewer of the book criticized us for not offering a "theory" of reading. Part III we called "Questions People Ask about Reading." These questions dealt with clinical or applied topics like dyslexia, "rapid reading," how parents can help children, and so on. We called our book *The Psychology of Reading* (Gibson and Levin, 1975).

My views on reading changed radically during the years I worked on it. I thought of reading rather simplistically at first, as requiring learning to discriminate phonemes and graphemes, and decoding one system to another (which it does, of course). But I became more and more impressed by the structure in the text and by the importance of the reader's task, which is necessarily variable, depending on what one is reading and why. I quote again the conclusion of one of the last colloquia I gave on reading:

> Mature reading is marked by discovery of structure; by use of structure and
> rules to achieve economy of performance and by adapting information

pickup to the reader's task. The difference between a reader who uses the redundancy given by all these kinds of structure efficiently and automatically, and a beginning scholar who is presumed to stumble along decoding letter by letter into speech sounds cannot be exaggerated. The accomplishment of reading and comprehending the text of "War and Peace" is as wonderful as reading the score of a symphony, which does not come through note by note any more than the former comes through letter by letter.(E. J. Gibson, 1991, p. 472)

Still, one never finishes thinking about a problem and feels totally satisfied. I now think we did not stress enough that one reads for meaning; furthermore, meaning that has a use for oneself. I believe one should teach children (insofar as they can be taught by someone else to read) with that aim in mind from the start. It helps a child learn to read on his or her own, which is the only way one learns to read skillfully.

Meanwhile, my husband had begun to think about his last and most important book (I say this although his books were all important and ground-breaking). Ever since 1966, when *The Senses Considered as Perceptual Systems* was published, James had been pushing his perceptual theory into still newer territory. He had not at that time totally given up the traditional notion of the retinal image as the foundation of visual perception, but soon afterward, he did. He no longer wanted to rely so heavily on the idea of correspondence with higher order variables (although that concept did not disappear). Most important, he gave major emphasis to a new concept that he called *affordance*. The word was actually introduced earlier in his 1966 book, but he had since come to think of it as a major concept of his theory of perception. In 1966 he wrote:

> I have coined this word as a substitute for *values*, a term which carries an old burden of philosophical meaning. I mean simply what things furnish, for good or ill. What they *afford* the observer, after all, depends on their properties. The simplest affordances, as food, for example, or as a predatory enemy, may well be detected without learning by the young of some animals, but in general learning is all-important for this kind of perception.(J. J. Gibson, 1966, p. 285)

Little more was said about affordances in that book, but now it was to become central to his thinking, the focus of a new, very radical way of thinking about perception, which he called the *ecological approach*.

The new theory, as it grew, was so radical indeed that he spent the rest of his life working on it. He would retire to his study every evening immediately after dinner and work there far into the night. In the introduction to his new (and last) book, he said:

> This book is a sequel to "The Perception of the Visual World" which came out in 1950. It is rather different, however, because my explanation of vision was then based on the retinal image, whereas it is now based on what I call the ambient optic array. I now believe we must take an ecological approach to the problems of perception. (J. J. Gibson, 1979, p. 1)

The new approach to perception is manifest in the very organization of the book. Part I (there are four parts) is titled "The Environment to Be Perceived." It begins with a chapter on the animal and the environment, which stresses the mutuality of animal and environment, that each one implicates the other. The environment, for an animal, is not the environment of physics, but a layout of surfaces and objects appropriate to the scale of the animal. It is structured, but events taking place in the environment may involve change of structure. Every animal is a perceiver and a behaver. An animal is a perceiver of the environment and behaves in it, in accordance with what the environment affords it; reciprocally, the animal's behavior changes the environment.

Part II is called "The Information for Visual Perception" and includes five chapters, one of them on the optical information for self-perception. The final chapter here is on the theory of affordances and includes a now famous statement:

> The information to specify the utilities of the environment is accompanied by information to specify the observer himself, his body, legs, hands, and mouth. This is only to reemphasize that exteroception is accompanied by proprioception—that to perceive the world is to co-perceive oneself. (p. 141)

The information for this is indeed a high-level invariant.

Part III of the book is "Visual Perception." This is a very meaty section, very functional in emphasis, and it contains a wealth of experimental evidence from the prior 35 years of James's research. Illustrations designed by James for this section or taken from one or another of his research papers have been copied in countless texts. Most impressive is a chapter titled "Locomotion and Manipulation." His revolutionary discovery of the importance of flow patterns in the ambient optic array, now universally accepted, finds its proper place here. James's own copy of the book is filled with notes in this section, indicating new ideas emerging that, alas, he did not have time to complete and carry further. There is a discussion here, in chapter 14, of knowing and perceiving, a vital topic.

Boring was no longer alive to review James's last book. What a pity! The contrast with Boring's narrow view of perception is almost inconceivable. Boring (1933) wrote that

> A complete knowledge of the psychology of sensory data would be an approximately complete knowledge of consciousness. The sensory data are organized in respect to at least four conscious dimensions: quality, intensity, extensity, and protensity. We have nothing to seek further than the full account of mental organization in respect of these dimensions. (p. 31)

He also wrote that "The thesis of this book is that nothing is 'directly observed'; that every fact is an implication'" (p. 30). What an impoverished venture he envisioned compared with the ecological approach!

I cite one review of this book, by Frank Restle, an esteemed experimentalist. Restle (1980) titled his review "The Seer of Ithaca." He wrote, "This book comes forth as a major theory, as the culmination of the life's work of Jimmy Gibson, our one original, irreplaceable creative genius" (p. 291). Sad to say, James never got to read this review, but at least he lived to see his book published and enthusiastically received by friends and followers.

Of course other things happened, too, while those books were being written. I haven't mentioned the honors both of us received. It doesn't make for very interesting reading, but I might as well include it for the record. My husband received The Howard Crosby Warren Medal (given by The Society of Experimental Psychologists) in 1952, soon after *The Visual World* came out. I received it too, but not until 1977. He was elected a member of the National Academy of Sciences in 1967, and so was I, in 1971. He received The Distinguished Contribution Award from the American Psychological Association in 1961 and I received it in 1968. We were both (one at a time, of course, and James always prior) elected President of the Eastern Psychological Association and of Division 3 of the American Psychological Association. I can remember only one of these occasions as outstanding in any way. The year that I was President of the Eastern Psychological Association, the annual meeting was held in Washington, DC at a large hotel, the Sheraton, and we were given (gratis) the royal suite (or so it looked, huge and grandiose). We proceeded to have a party in it, of memorable proportions—all our friends from other universities and quite a few uninvited guests. My sister came to dine with us before the party, walked in and said, "Holy cow!"

In 1972, I received my first honorary degree from Smith College, my respected and beloved alma mater. It was an exceptionally happy occasion, with old friends and parties. Smith at that time still had a male president, Tom Mendenhall, a kindly gray-haired gentleman of generous proportions. He was known to the students as "Uncle Tom." His mother, Dorothy Mendenhall, was a Smith alumna, well-known in her time. Since Mendenhall, Smith's presidents have always been women; distinguished ones, too.

During these years, two very welcome events happened for me. In 1972, Cornell made me the Susan Linn Sage Professor of Psychology. The Sage professorships (three of them) had always been held by philosophers, but this time, when a Sage Professor retired, the professorship was awarded to psychology. Max Black, a philosopher who held one, telephoned me and said, I thought rather sarcastically, "Welcome to the Sages." I saluted the Sage family indeed. The professorship had never been held by a woman before (despite the "Susan"). I'm not sure who Susan was, but the Sage family have been great benefactors of Cornell, being the donors of Sage Chapel, among other things.

The other welcome event was a new building, Uris Hall, built for the social sciences with two floors of large proportions designated for psychology. For the very first time, I was to have a lab of my own! I even had the opportunity to design it with the architect. I decided on an infant lab, which I had always wanted, and it totally changed my research outlook and program. I phased out the reading research and began planning studies on infant perception. My husband got a new perception lab, too, next to my space, including one very long room. All the experimental labs were in the basement of the building, with offices two floors above. My husband did not have long, however, to enjoy his new lab.

We did not stay at home all this time, either. In the spring of 1969, I was invited to give 10 lectures for Sigma Xi at 10 different sites in the Midwest, all one-night stands with a weekend in the middle. The trip was billed as "The Great Lakes Lecture Tour," starting with the University of Michigan. In most cases, my talk was presented in the late afternoon and then followed by the annual local Sigma Xi club banquet. The audience was a mixed group of scientists, not just psychologists. I also talked to eight undergraduate psychology clubs. The institutions ranged from Alma College, a small Presbyterian college in Alma, Michigan, to the Argonne National Laboratory, in Illinois. I talked on perceptual development, relating it to evolution as much as I could, and I used plenty of slides and colorful examples (E. J. Gibson, 1970a). I spent the weekend that divided the lectures at my mother's home in Peoria, Illinois. She was horrified at what I had undertaken, but it all went off satisfactorily and I met scientists in many other disciplines. I decided to undertake no more such tours, however.

In 1978, my husband had essentially finished writing *The Ecological Approach to Visual Perception* and we accepted an invitation to spend a term at the University of California at Davis. It was a good visit. The climate was kind to my husband, whose health was deteriorating, and we made some good friends. In the Psychology Department, there was Robert Sommer and his wife, another twosome of psychologists. Bob Sommer was a versatile character: he drew, wrote witty things, and was remarkably good at vetting ailing departments. He would be made temporary chairman of a department having problems, and hand it back after a year, good as new! Our greatest boon that term was the opportunity to make friends with Marjorie Grene, a member of the Philosophy Department. She was interested in James's ecological approach; she is exactly my age, to the day, and we have remained great friends into our 80s.

Our last visit away together was to the Salk Institute in La Jolla, California, in the spring of 1979. The invitation was arranged by Ursula Bellugi, a permanent fellow there. She had attended a memorial conference for Eric Lenneberg that was held at Cornell a year or so earlier. I had been assigned to comment on papers delivered by Bellugi and by Selma Fraiberg. Bellugi talked about language development in deaf children and Fraiberg about language development in blind children. I talked about the information that specifies "I" and how it differs in blind and deaf children (E. J. Gibson, 1991). Bellugi was interested and thought she and I might do some work to-

Fig. 17. James and Eleanor Gibson visiting at the University of California at San Diego, Winter 1979.

gether. That did not happen, as it turned out. James and I had offices with gorgeous views of the Pacific Ocean and the climate was truly benign. The intellectual environment was not especially congenial to us, however. One of the fellows, Francis Crick (of double helix fame) annoyed my husband greatly by announcing that he would be glad to solve all the problems of visual perception for him. It was thus not quite as healing an atmosphere as I had anticipated.

When we arrived home, my department held a surprise celebration for me on the first of June to mark my formal retirement (which had actually occurred somewhat earlier). It was a real celebration, with old students returning from all parts of the country. There was a luncheon, followed by a program of papers, all presented by my old graduate students talking about their current research (nine of them), and finally a party in the evening. It was an occasion to remember. My family came, too, making it a real reunion.

I have been neglecting our children in these last two chapters. They were, in fact, a source of constant joy and pride to us. Jerry graduated from Harvard in the early 1960s, still unsure of what he wanted to do with his life. The Peace Corps was new at the time, and like many other graduates he decided to join, giving himself a chance to see a new part of the world and time to consider plans for the future. It was the right decision. He was sent to Nyasaland (soon to be Malawi) to teach in a boarding high school for children who came in from remote jungle areas. He taught science, math, and English! He had majored in science and was good at math, so that part worked well. When he was assigned to teach French also, I was dubious about the quality of the teaching! When the school had vacations, he rode a bicycle through the jungle and visited the homes of his students, frequently spending the night. He wrote after one of these visits, "Roast pumpkin for dinner! Yum!" He was exceedingly impressed by the extent of disease in the country, at least some of which could have been controlled by public health measures. One such endemic disease was bilharzia, contracted by walking barefoot in shallow water where small snails carried the infection.

He made up his mind, after a year of this, that his future should be in disease control, so his next step had to be medical school. He managed the incredible (to me) feat of applying to medical schools from Malawi, getting the forms, recommendations, and so on, off to four schools. Cornell Medical School did not even grant him an interview, to his father's indignation, but he was accepted by the Medical School of the University of Pittsburgh, which subsequently gave him a fine medical education and where he met his future wife, Lois Rauch (a graduate student in English literature). After medical school and internships, he spent time with the Centers for Disease Control and the World Health Organization and traveled to Kosovo and Northern India helping to eradicate smallpox. Now he is the state epidemiologist for South Carolina, a job he enjoys and performs magnificently.

Our daughter Jean attended Smith College after finishing Northfield, and after graduation, to our great pleasure, returned to Cornell to attend graduate school in economics. We did not see as much of her as we had hoped, however, because she chose to live in an apartment in the graduate student slums in College Town. But of course, there were trips home with laundry and occasionally for meals. We met her friends, one of whom, David Rosenberg, she married before they traveled to the Philippines for dissertation research. David's field is political science, and he was fortunate to be appointed assistant professor at Middlebury College in Vermont in 1972. Jean taught economics for a few years at the University of Vermont, until she found that economics was boring her and turned to other interests that are more in line with her social concerns and with the philosophy of the Society of Friends (Quakers), to which she belongs.

I finish this chapter on a happy note, weddings. Jean's took place outdoors in 1969, in our own wonderful backyard. We built a small wooden pergola near the back of the yard, which sloped downward. The ceremony was performed there, and there was a jolly sort of tent canopy near the house over a table holding refreshments. The groom's brother was best man. His parents and other relatives came, as did my mother and sister and a number of our relatives. Of course there were numerous graduate students, too (happy, among other things, with the lavish refreshments). It was a splendid, beautiful occasion and I never saw my husband look happier, even as he gave his beloved daughter away. The following year, Jerry married Lois Rauch, only 1 month into his internship. He was given 1 day off from his clinical service for the honeymoon. The wedding was a real contrast to Jean's, held in New York in a large ballroom. The relatives all came and we danced at the wedding.

10

The Seer of Ithaca[1]

I'd like to begin this chapter on a cheerful note, so I'll continue with a little more history of the children. Jean and David, the first to be married, also presented us with our first grandchild, Eli, born in 1972. He was a handsome baby, and needless to say, we were pleased as punch, proud grandparents indeed. Middlebury, their home, is an easy drive from Ithaca, so we visited there and watched him grow, and they often brought him to visit us. His sister, Elizabeth, was born in 1977, bringing us further happiness.

Jerry and Lois stayed in New York for 1 year while Jerry did his internship on the Columbia University service at Harlem Hospital, which afforded plenty of patient responsibility. He then joined the Epidemic Intelligence Service of the Centers for Disease Control (CDC) in Atlanta, and he was sent to his first post at the Arkansas State Health Department. Then followed 2 years in Atlanta at CDC's Parasitic Disease Branch. Residency in internal medicine followed at the University of Oregon. There Michael, our second grandson, was born in 1977, a few months before his cousin Elizabeth. We

---

[1] I have borrowed this title from Frank Restle, whose title it was for his review of James's last book (Restle, 1980).

hurried to Portland to see the new baby and were left in charge of him when he was only 1 week old while his parents went to the registry of births to change the spelling of his middle name from Steven to Stephen at our request. We sat outdoors in the pleasant Oregon summer and I held him in my arms the whole time. I give these details because it is such a pleasure to remember them and to rejoice in the fact that my husband had the opportunity to be acquainted with these three wonderful grandchildren.

After Michael and Elizabeth's births, the opportunities grew fewer, because James's health began deteriorating. The time in California at the Salk Institute in the spring of 1979 was our last long visit away. He had become ill with cancer before that and stoically withstood chemotherapy, but he grew weaker in the summer that followed, and in the late fall very ill, eventually requiring hospitalization. The problem was pancreatic cancer, and it was hopeless. I spent every day at the hospital, and sad days they were. The family, including Jerry and Lois, visited briefly when they could. One day in early December the doctor said to me, "You need someone in your family here with you, now!" I telephoned Jean and asked her to come, arranging for a small plane that could be hired at the Ithaca airport to fly to Middlebury and bring her to Ithaca. She had to bring along little Elizabeth, bewildered by the situation. James died on December 11, only 3 days later.

We arranged a memorial service to be held in Sage Chapel about a week later, giving family, relatives, and friends time to make arrangements to be present. My brother-in-law, William Gibson, insisted that the congregation sing "Integer Vitae," sung traditionally when the Gibson family was together. It was not in the chapel's hymn book, and none of us remembered all the words, but a friend in another department, Robert Hall, found the words in an old Latin text. We made copies, and graduate students handed them out at the chapel doors as people entered. Three friends spoke at the service: Ulric Neisser, a colleague; Robert Shaw, a psychologist at the University of Connecticut who was an ardent advocate of James's "ecological approach"; and Henry Gleitman, psychologist at the University of Pennsylvania and a longtime friend.

It was a memorable service, and friends called afterward at our home on Oak Hill Road. When most of the guests had gone and only family remained, one of my brothers-in-law said, "Now, it's time to make some memorial side-cars." James had been noted in the family for this potent concoction, a combination of brandy, triple sec, and lemon juice. I even remember what we had for dinner afterward. I had made, ahead of time, two huge casseroles of seafood tetrazzini, The children probably got something else. The younger two had been consigned to babysitters for the afternoon, but we had taken Eli, now 7 years old, to the service. I remember his saying, "This is very sad, Grandma." But it wasn't really sad, it was a good remembrance.

Sadness came when they had all gone home, and I was truly alone. I was not the only one who was sad at losing James. There was his family, of course, but also his departmental colleagues, graduate students, his older now-established students, and a growing body of young and vigorous psychologists who were won over by his new approach to perception, the ecological approach as he called it. Two notable things happened as a consequence. Art and Mary Ryan, our longtime friends and colleagues at Cornell, suggested that a lectureship be founded in James's memory. Friends and family gave generously to fund this memorial, now known as the James J. Gibson Lecture in Experimental Psychology. The first lecture was given by James's dear friend, Gunnar Johansson, who came from Uppsala, Sweden, in October 1981, to speak on "Optic Flow and Visual Perception," a topic that had commanded their united interest. The lectures continue annually on varied topics in experimental psychology.

Of even greater significance was the founding of the International Society for Ecological Psychology. More and more psychologists had been attracted by James's radical new approach to the study of perception. Among them were some very enthusiastic, active young people who saw great virtue in

Fig. 18. The seer of Ithaca.

establishing a group that others could join, that would hold meetings where they could report their research and hold discussions, and that would publish a journal where their views could be aired and shared with other psychologists. The founders of this group included William Mace of Trinity College in Hartford; David Lee of the University of Edinburgh; Robert Shaw and Michael Turvey of the University of Connecticut; Carol Fowler of Dartmouth College; Edward Reed, a young philosopher at Franklin and Marshall College; Sverker Runeson of Uppsala University; and others who eagerly joined in (and joined up!). There was a foundation of James's old loyal graduate students to draw on, for starters. The journal, *Ecological Psychology*, appears four times a year and is about to complete Volume 11. There have been a number of highly successful congresses, drawing an international audience, held not only in the United States but in Canada (Vancouver and Toronto) and most recently in Edinburgh, in the summer of 1999. All of the contributors stress the reciprocity between perception and action, and action has become a big topic, but so is the concept of affordance, the heart of James's theory of perception, showing how perception relates to action. Locomotion has always been a big topic in ecological psychology, and recently a special issue of the journal (Vol. 10, 1998) was devoted to the topic. It was a commemoration of James's 1958 article, "Visually Controlled Locomotion and Visual Orientation in Animals and Man" (J. J. Gibson, 1958), an important paper that foreshadowed his later insistence on the essential relation between an animal and its environment. The paper was reprinted and a number of new, original papers on locomotion accompanied it. The issue was edited by William Warren, of Brown University, a leader of the new generation of ecological psychologists.

Other tributes occurred in the form of books. Some of James's old friends, colleagues, and students paid him an impressive tribute, a festschrift titled *Perception: Essays in Honor of James J. Gibson*. The editors were Robert MacLeod and Herbert Pick. MacLeod died before the volume was ready for publication, but not before he had worked on the plan and written a foreword. The book is divided into two sections. Part I is called "Gibson and the Perceptual World." The roster of authors of the essays is international (an indication of MacLeod's influence), including Julian Hochberg, Mary Henle, Wolfgang Metzger (German), Kai von Fieandt (Finnish), E. H. Gombrich (British), Fabio Metelli (Italian), and Gunnar Johansson (Swedish). These scholars were all friends of many years. Part II is called "Gibson and the Perceptual Field." The authors were of a younger generation, some James's students, and others young psychologists who had been influenced by his views. There were essays by Tom Bower, Herbert Pick, Jacob Beck, Howard Flock, John

Kennedy, John Hay (all of them James's students), David Lee, Y. B. Gippenreiter, V. Y. Romanov, Robert Shaw, Michael MacIntyre, and William Mace. Even in this group there are some Europeans, such as the two Russians and David Lee. The collection of these essays began not long after the publication in 1966 of James's book, *The Senses Considered as Perceptual Systems* (J. J. Gibson, 1966), so the topics tend toward the nature of the information that specifies what is perceived, especially the essays in Part II, which are generally more research oriented than those of Part I. The charm of MacLeod's brief remarks about his friend brings home sharply what we have lost in these two men. The book was presented to James in 1974 at a party, where as many as possible of the authors were gathered. The invitations read "You are invited to a Festschrift." But we didn't write at the party.

Later books of importance were two biographies of James Gibson. One of these was preceded by a volume, *Reasons for Realism*, edited by Edward Reed and Rebecca Jones, a collected edition of a number of James's more important papers (Reed & Jones, 1982), and a complete bibliography of his work. James had agreed to this collection before his death, but did not live to witness its publication. The book contains not only previously published papers, but also unpublished material, including an edited version of James's opening remarks for a workshop on ecological optics held at Cornell University in June 1970. The paper, entitled "A History of the Ideas Behind Ecological Optics: Introductory Remarks at the Workshop on Ecological Optics," was put together by two of the participants, Anthony Barrand and Mike Riegel.

In 1988, Ed Reed published a biography, *James J. Gibson and the Psychology of Perception* (Reed, 1988). This biography is both personal and academic, describing important incidents in James's life as well as following his changing ideas. Reed spent many weeks in the archives of Olin Library at Cornell, where James's papers are deposited, in researching this biography. Reed was very sympathetic to both James as a person and to his ideas. He presented a complete and affectionate picture (plus a few of his own personal interpretations of James's motives!). Ed Reed later wrote several other books, philosophical works related to the principles of ecological psychology. Sadly, he died in 1997 of a sudden heart attack, much too young and at the height of his powers.

The second biography of James Gibson was written by one of his former graduate students, Thomas Lombardo. Actually, Tom Lombardo was a graduate student at the University of Minnesota, where he came under the tutelage of two older one-time students of James's, Herbert Pick and Robert Shaw. Lombardo learned from them about Gibson's radical ideas about perception and was greatly attracted to them. He was especially interested in the philosophical implications underlying these ideas, and eventually suggested that he write his dissertation on Gibson's ideas and how they evolved. The suggestion was accepted, and in 1972, Tom Lombardo received a fellowship from the Center for Research in Human Learning at Minnesota to spend a year studying with James at Cornell. He finished his dissertation in 1973, before *The Ecological Approach to Visual Perception* (J. J. Gibson, 1979) was completed and published. The dissertation focussed on Gibson's psychophysical theories and his eschewal of elementarism. However, Tom later received a postdoctoral fellowship in 1979 to study at the University of Connecticut, which now counted both Robert Shaw and Michael Turvey on its faculty. At that time, Tom's dissertation was reorganized and rewritten, so as to include the more recent ideas in Gibson's ecological approach. Lombardo eventually completed and published his biography in 1987, calling it *The Reciprocity of Perceiver and Environment: The Evolution of James J. Gibson's Ecological Psychology* (Lombardo, 1987). This work is greatly concerned with epistemology, and many chapters are devoted to the philosophical background of Gibson's ideas. The emphasis is entirely theoretical, in no way duplicating Reed's biography.

I include a paragraph from the Cornell University Memorial Statement, prepared by James's close friends, Harry Levin, Thomas A. Ryan, and Ulric Neisser. They wrote:

Gibson called his theory An Ecological Approach to Visual Perception; this was the title of his last book, which appeared in 1979 a few months before his death. It was an ecological approach as opposed to a mentalistic or mechanistic or neurological one. He felt that the proper study of vision must begin with an analysis of the light available to the eye, with an "ecological optics," not with the postulation of hypothetical mental processes and not with extrapolation from fragmentary neurophysiological findings. This position put him increasingly at odds with prevailing trends in his field. In his last years he occupied a peculiar position in that field, being simultaneously its most eminent and most dissident member. But he was not alone: a "Gibsonian" intellectual movement has been gathering strength for more than a decade. It is now recognized in both psychology and philosophy as a major alternative to established views of the nature and acquisition of knowledge. If the leaders of that movement are to follow J. J. Gibson's example, they will have to be intellectually unyielding and yet unfailingly courteous to those of other persuasions, highly imaginative and yet closely attentive to the most ordinary experiences of daily life, at once determinedly experimental and deeply theo-

retical. A reviewer of his last book called Gibson "our one original, irreplaceable creative genius." And so he was.

I have said very little about the kind of partnership that my husband and I
evolved over our 47 years of married life. The nature of the bond between
us was a major reason for my deciding to write this memoir. We were never
a husband-and-wife team, nor was I a long-suffering wife who gave up a
teaching career in order to further her husband's, or to devote herself primarily to tending to her family (as did Lucy May Boring, one of the first women to
be awarded a degree in psychology). It is true that James was 7 years my senior, was my teacher in an undergraduate class, and was the professor who
directed my master's thesis. All this made him greatly my superior in wisdom
and in professional knowledge. He had publications and friends in the profession that commanded my respect, as did his ideas and his ingenuity in
thinking up and planning experiments. But he thought he saw a creative
spark in me, too. When it came time for me to go away somewhere to study
for a PhD, he left the decision entirely up to me. His own field of expertise
was perception. I chose to apply to Yale, where there was not one person on
the faculty who worked on or even cared about perception. The focus of attention at Yale was on learning, the stylish topic of the day. This was not only
true of the older faculty, such as Clark Hull and E. R. Robinson, but of the
younger members too, notably Donald Marquis and Neal Miller, already
recognized in the field.

Moreover, my husband was due for his first sabbatical leave the year that I
took off for New Haven. He could only afford one semester away, and he
might have spent that semester at a European university or at Harvard, say.
But he didn't; he joined me in New Haven the second semester, and even
taught a small class for the privilege of occupying an office there. Of course it
wasn't wasted time; he wrote things up, made a preliminary test of an idea
for a new experiment, and we kept in close touch with each other. The difference between his ideas and Clark Hull's (my Yale mentor) could scarcely
have been greater, but this was tolerated by both. He made new friends. I re-
call this time, because it shows that the many times that I "went along" wher-
ever he was going were not an exceptional sacrifice and that we began both
our married and our professional lives respecting each other's choices and
the need for freedom to think on our own.

Having made this point clear (I hope), I now must admit that despite all
this freedom to think as we pleased, we did in fact influence one another.
Even my choice of Yale was influenced in a way. James was already a func-
tionalist, differing profoundly from the traditional structuralist, Titchenerian

stance of most perception psychologists. He had been influenced by his mentor, E. B. Holt, I believe. Holt considered himself a radical empiricist, a term he took from William James. One of Holt's books is titled *Animal Drive and the Learning Process: An Essay Toward Radical Empiricism* (Holt, 1931). There is much talk in the book about reflexes, and the terms *adaptation* and *evolution* are not even in the index, so Holt's was not a very modern form of functionalism. But he stated that "behavior is not a function of the immediate stimulus" (Holt, 1915, p. 164) and that behavior "remains a function of some object, process, or aspect of the objective environment" (p. 165). He was discussing behavior, not sensations, and he referred to behavior as a process, worlds away from the views of either structuralism or reflexology. This functional view influenced my choice of Yale, where behavior was a topic of study.

Both my husband and I took pride in any award or recognition given the other. I accompanied him as a matter of course to Uppsala and to Edinburgh when he received honorary degrees at these ancient and hallowed universities. He, for his part, accompanied me to Northampton, Massachusetts, when in 1972 Smith College awarded me the degree of Honorary Doctor of Science. The occasion itself was delightful, preceded the evening before by a cocktail party at a friend's home, a dinner given by the president of the college, and finally a dance. I think James enjoyed it as much as I did.

I mentioned in a previous chapter a festschrift prepared in honor of my husband. I was the lucky recipient of one, too, edited by my old student and good friend Anne Pick (1979). It was published in 1979, but the essays were written somewhat earlier, and one (the foreword) was contributed by my husband. I quote a bit from it, because it tells a great deal about our relationship and how the vicissitudes of accommodating two careers in the same profession and family did not destroy our enjoyment in our life together, nor the family:

> Back at Smith, where the faculty was half male and half female, the unconscious prejudice against women was scarcely noticeable. She might have had an academic career there, since the insidious danger of nepotism was not sternly prohibited, as it was at the universities. But the War interfered. In 1940 she was an assistant professor with a full schedule, a fine old house to live in, a housekeeper with standards, a male baby, and an admiring husband. But she gave it all up, save for the last two. The husband was sent to Texas where the flying training for the Air Corps was concentrated, and she took the baby and went along without question, for she liked her family as much as her profession, and she never saw any reason why she should not have both.... (J. J. Gibson, 1979, p. x)

So for 5 long years she had a household, another baby, and a stay-at-home life, with food and gas rationing to cope with. The community at Fort Worth, Texas was not stimulating, and that at Santa Ana, California near the Air Base, was so reactionary as to be stifling. Whereas her husband was doing psychological research that, luckily for him, was full of interest, she could only mark time. (J. J. Gibson, 1979, p. xi)

But we returned to Smith, as I have explained, and then moved to Cornell, where (with some struggle), I managed to have a career of sorts in research, occasionally collaborating on some work with my husband, but mostly on separate topics of my own choice. Here is what he had to say about that:

What was the relationship between her work and mine over all these years? My judgment is even less to be trusted on that score, one would suppose, and yet it is a fair question. She has a separate but related body of research and publication, and she began it under the influence of Hull. We have collaborated on occasion but not as a regular thing. And when we did, we were not a husband-and-wife "team," God knows, for we argued endlessly. The popular concept of a married pair of scientists working harmoniously together is a sentimental stereotype in which the wife is a "helper." We have been influenced by somewhat different trends in psychology and somewhat different people, but not different enough to make us go in separate ways. We have always read the same books even if we did not agree about them, and each of us has always influenced the other more than anyone else did. (J. J. Gibson, p. xii)

There are two points to be emphasized in that paragraph. One, when we collaborated on some paper, especially on a theoretical one, we did indeed argue, even at the dinner table, as our children are still reminding me! The result was usually worth the battle, however. The work we did together was good and to this day I am proud of it. We could write a "Reply to Professor Postman" (J. J. Gibson & E. J. Gibson, 1955b) or a "Reply to Professor Gregory" (E. J. Gibson & J. J. Gibson, 1972) and set down a whale of an argument, with conclusions on which we concurred.

The other point is the one about influence. That my husband's ideas influenced me is unquestionable and obvious. True, I chose Hull as a dissertation advisor and applied principles of conditioning to verbal learning. However, the principles I chose were relevant to perception—generalization and differentiation—and in the end my husband and I used the concepts (especially differentiation) as the foundation for a theory of perceptual learning. Later, his concept of affordances became the focus of my research on perceptual development in infants. Indeed it is the prevailing theoretical notion in my thinking about perceptual learning in my most recent book (E. J. Gibson & Pick, 2000). Not only did our marriage survive the arguments; I, the survivor, am still pushing ideas I took from him many years after his death.

The conclusion is that a woman can indeed have both a family and a career, if her companion is the right kind of guy. She should not worry about making concessions to his career if she has her own thoughts and ambitions clearly in mind. Her time comes, too, and the rewards for all can be great.

11

Going It Alone

My family spent Christmas with me after my husband's death, but then it was time for me to stand on my own feet and face the future. I had two things going for me, my lab and my old friends. First came the lab, the hard-won, superb lab for which I had waited so long. Although I had to retire at the age of 65 from the teaching faculty, my department and the university were glad to have me continue my research, because I was able to attract good graduate students and bring in grant money to support the lab and several graduate assistants. It cost them nothing, while adding prestige and another advisor for graduate students. It was evidently not against the rules for an emeritus professor to oversee and evaluate dissertation research, or, of course, to give a seminar, as my husband had done for 10 years after his retirement, and I intended to carry on the tradition.

My laboratory was planned for conducting research on infants, which I had always wanted to do, and it was used accordingly as soon as it was completed. Elizabeth Spelke, one of my best-ever students (and a friend), was the earliest to carry out dissertation research there. She devised a method of studying bimodal perception in infants that aroused great attention among developmental psychologists (Spelke, 1976). She showed babies filmed events, exposed side by side on a screen, accompanied by the soundtrack for just one of them. Where would the babies look? Either way? Or at the one that presented them with a unified event? Looking was carefully monitored and the result was clear. The babies watched the film that accompanied the sound- track. A number of experiments have verified this result.

The experiments that inaugurated my lab were focused on infant percep- tion, but not perception of geometric forms such as squares and circles or even pictures, as many of the early experiments had been. We studied the in- fants' perception of real objects and their properties, such as their rigidity or flexibility—a very important property, because people exhibit animate, flexi- ble movements, such as smiles and expressions of distress (E. J. Gibson, Owsley & Johnston, 1978). This property was investigated in a number of experiments with my graduate students, including Cynthia Owsley, Arlene Walker, Lorraine Bahrick, and others.

All of us in my lab group were very interested in multimodal perception. Information for perception, from the start, is never confined in any event to a single modality, such as vision. The very earliest visual observation or haptic exploration of an event or object brings with it proprioceptive information. A turn of the head, sucking, or kicking, for example, all bring information about what is going on in one's own body. Arlene Walker and I (E. J. Gibson & Walker, 1984) performed an experiment on detecting the correspondence of haptic and visually obtained information for the rigidity or flexibility of ob- ject substance. Infants of 1 month were first given either a spongy or a hard object to explore orally. After a period of habituation they were presented with two live performances to observe visually. In one of them, a circular ob- ject of sponge rubber was moved in a deforming motion; in the other, an ob- ject of the same shape and size was moved in a rigid motion. The infants demonstrated recognition of the motion characteristic of the object they had mouthed by looking preferentially at the novel type of movement. Informa- tion about rigidity or flexibility can thus be obtained either visually or haptically. Either way, information is provided about the affordance of an object's substance.

Studying development of perception of the affordances of things, places or events was a major theme of the work in my laboratory. The concept of affordance was the major theme of my husband's ecological theory of per- ception, and I wanted to study the way perception of affordances develops, for I am now convinced that what is learned in perceptual learning is the affordances of things, layout, or whatever the infant encounters. Learning for nearly the whole first year of life occurs without language or explicit teaching. The baby is on his or her own to observe and explore, in any way he or she can, whatever is present in the near environment. As motor skills develop during the first year (reaching, handling objects, sitting, crawling, walking) more and more about what the world affords can be learned. The learning occurs spontaneously and eagerly and provides a foundation of knowledge for the lessons in language that will come later.

A second kind of perception we studied was learning about the surfaces of things, especially what surfaces in the layout afford for locomotion as babies begin to move about on their own. What surfaces can be safely sat on, crawled on, or walked on? My old research on the visual cliff had provoked an interest in how infants come to perceive affordances of the layout for going somewhere, and now I had the means of carrying the research further. What about going around obstacles and through passages? What about moving onto an unfamiliar surface ahead?

Experiments on mobility and perceiving the affordances of layout were performed a little later than most of the experiments on perceiving properties and affordances of objects. A major reason for this was the need for allotting a great deal of laboratory space for the equipment needed. Eventually we built a large walkway and a moving room, patterned after David Lee's original one (Lee & Aronson, 1974). We could do this after my husband's death because we fell heir to his laboratory space, which was next to mine. I progressed from having no laboratory of my own to having a very large one in a period of 7 or 8 years.

My first experiment on layout perception in infants was done with John Carroll on differentiation of an obstacle from an aperture by 3-month-old infants. We wondered whether preambulatory infants would detect the difference between an area that would afford passage and an area of similar proportions that would obstruct them so as to produce collision if contacted. We measured the infants' head pressure against a headrest containing pressure transducers, reasoning that an aperture moving toward the infant would provide no threat of collision, whereas a solid structure of the same size would, and might therefore induce head retraction if the infant perceived the affordance. Despite the absence of mobility, learning the different affordances of an aperture and an obstacle might be possible as the infant is conveyed around the environment. Although moving oneself in the layout would of course be more informative, especially in terms of consequences, the optic flow patterns induced by the two experimental conditions would be quite different from one another and could attract notice. The infants did, in fact, show avoidance behavior only to the moving obstacle. This experiment and the others following are summarized in a comprehensive paper on mobility by E. J. Gibson and Schmuckler (1989).

The major problems of motility needing developmental study were suggested by J. J. Gibson's (1979a) discussion of locomotion: (a) describing the information for the traveler's selection of a path, (b) evaluation of the terrain for traversability, and (c) maintenance of postural stability. There is multimodal information obtainable for all of these, with vision and the optic flow patterns induced by movement heading the list. All three of these problems received attention in my infant laboratory, opening up a vast field for research by developmental psychologists. The first problem was addressed in the aperture–obstacle experiment, and then we proceeded to the other two.

Discovering the traversability of a surface—whether or not it affords support and provides a safe ground for locomotion, was a question that engaged me particularly, and I set out to study its development with a wonderful crew of graduate students (see E. J. Gibson, et al., 1987). The old work on the visual cliff inspired the creation of a "walkway," although this time there was no cliff. There was a starting surface covered with burlap at one end, where the infants were first placed; this gave onto a broad area where surfaces with different visual and textural properties could be placed and compared. A parent stood at the far end opposite the baby, urging the child to come.

Our first experiment, inspired by our experiments on detection of the affordance of substances, was a comparison of a rigid versus a deforming surface. We observed the babies' exploratory activities, expressions of interest or avoidance, latency, whether they moved onto the surface, and of course their method of locomotion (if any). We were especially interested in a comparison of crawling versus walking infants. The rigid surface was constructed of firm plywood, covered with a cross-hatch pattern of brown and white. The deformable surface consisted of a waterbed, covered with the same material as the rigid surface and agitated gently from below. It provided perfectly safe support, but was not traversable by walking. Crawlers explored the surfaces less than walkers and moved onto the two surfaces with about equal latency. Walkers frequently stood up and crossed the rigid surface upright, but if they crossed the waterbed at all, they did so crawling. That they made use of haptic information about the deformable surface was made clear by a control experiment in which the surfaces were covered with transparent plexiglas. The waterbed was agitated to present optical evidence for deformability. This time, the walkers walked across the visible waterbed equally, detecting the surface's actual rigidity. Other surface features, such as limitation of visually obtainable information or presence of a hole revealing the floor below, were investigated, and suggested overall that infants of walking age, at least, deliberately seek information for a traversable surface, explore its affordance, and make use of the information.

The third big problem, how maintenance of postural stability is informed and how its maintenance develops, was addressed in experiments with a moving room. Earlier research with adults by Stoffregen had shown that optical flow that controls maintenance of stance is concentrated in flow patterns emanating from the periphery, as contrasted with patterns of frontal flow. It is possible that central radial flow is of prime utility for steering around obstacles and keeping on a path, whereas peripheral flow specifies staggering or wavering as one moves, thus warning of imbalance. Might this differentiation be learned in the course of locomotion during the early years? Appropriate experiments were carried out with two groups of children: a younger group, all walking but under 2 years of age, and an older group between 2 and 5 years old. Children in the younger group were more susceptible to flow information in general, easily losing postural stability at any room movement, but most significantly they had not yet fully differentiated central radial as contrasted with peripheral optic flow (Stoffregen, Schmuckler, & Gibson, 1987).

My research provided a constant source of interest and occupation for me, but I had another source of help and diversion. A few months after my husband's death, I received an invitation from Herbert and Anne Pick, both my old graduate students and one-time research assistants, to spend a quarter as visiting professor at the University of Minnesota, now their home base. They were afraid that I would be lonesome and forlorn by myself. I accepted, and spent the fall quarter of 1980 on their campus, enjoying the change of scene.

Next year, during the winter of 1981, I had a still greater change of scene at the University of South Carolina in Columbia. My son and daughter-in-law lived in Columbia now, and I had a fourth grandchild there, their son Jonathan, a baby whose acquaintance I was happy to make. The university offered me an adjunct professorship and an office, which I gladly accepted. That was the beginning of a long relationship with that university, for I have spent time there nearly every winter since then. They have always provided space for me and one year gave me an honorary degree! I made friends in the Psychology Department; became reacquainted with Lois and Abe Wandersman, old Cornell PhDs in developmental psychology; and had the advantage of another good friend, Karl Heider, in the nearby Department of Anthropology. Karl is the son of my old Northampton friends, Grace and Fritz Heider. He and his wife have in turn become good friends with Jerry and Lois, and the Heider and Gibson grandchildren are friends as well. It has become a family tradition for us to gather for Christmas dinner.

That was not the end of my traveling. In the fall of 1982 I was invited with two other psychologists, Rochel Gelman and Lauren Resnick, to spend a month at the University of Beijing, China, each of us to give an intensive seminar in our specialties to a small group of mature psychologists. The days of the Cultural Revolution were over, although our Chinese friends still wore Mao suits. They had all been exiled to the country for long periods and now at last released, felt an urgent need to fill in the gap and get back on the academic track. We three Americans were put up in comfortable rooms at the Friendship Hotel (run by the Chinese government) and provided with excellent meals. I had a car and driver to take me to the meeting with my group, with whom I became very good friends. I had to speak in English, of course, and their English was rusty and imperfect, but I put everything I could on the blackboard and we communicated pretty well. One of my group invited us to his tiny apartment for dinner one night. Dinner, cooked by his wife, was very good and it was a happy occasion. I was sure I would see these friends again, perhaps at a meeting in the United States, but I never have.

In 1984, my old student and friend Elizabeth Spelke, now a member of the faculty at the University of Pennsylvania, arranged an invitation for me to spend a term there as visiting professor. Other old friends, Henry and Lila Gleitman, are professors there, and again I enjoyed the change and the very collegial company. Liz and I together wrote a chapter on perceptual development for a handbook about that time. It was fun to do and gave us an excuse to visit back and forth. Arlene Walker-Andrews, another old graduate student, and I wrote a section on bimodal perception for an invited symposium. Joining my old students in projects like this has been one of the pleasures and rewards of my later years.

I mention one more excursion to a university, before I made a big change in my life. In 1986, I was invited to Dartmouth College for a term as the Montgomery Professor. This is a prestigious endowed professorship that passes annually from one department to another and carries various perquisites with it, a major one being a very large and handsome house on a pond near the campus. The house had a number of bedrooms and five bathrooms, so it easily housed multiple guests. Needless to say, I had them, especially Jean and David and their two children, as Middlebury, Vermont, their home, is an easy drive from Darthmouth. Each grandchild could bring a friend, because space was so ample. One remarkable feature of the house was an enormous, 8-foot-tall cloth sculpture of a woman (we think), that adorned the landing of a great staircase in the front hall. This work, presumably presented by a former guest or possibly by an alumnus, was rather terrifying to come on unexpectedly and caused dogs to erupt in fits of frantic barking. I thoroughly enjoyed the time there, partly because my friend Carol Fowler, a member of the ecological psychology group, was a professor at

Dartmouth. Other ecological psychologists visited at my remarkable house, making it a pleasant and profitable stay.

One winter during a visit to South Carolina my son announced that he had purchased a lot on Fripp Island, an island on the South Carolina coast somewhere between Charleston and Hilton Head. This island was not as yet highly developed and it seemed a good opportunity to acquire a family vacation house. Jerry could not afford to build a house as well as buy the lot, so I became a partner and we planned a fine cottage. The lot is not on the ocean, but it is only a 5-minute walk from it. Our house faces a tidal canal visited by many birds, especially white egrets and an occasional blue heron. The view of the canal and its changing tides is delightful, and the many palmetto trees and live oaks on the lot provide cover for deer that cross the canal at low tide. The house has a large living-dining room with a counter separating it from a generous kitchen. Bar stools at the counter are great places to feed the children. There is a screened porch at one side and a deck all across the front facing the canal. The children were quite young when we built the house and thoroughly enjoyed the beach, digging in the sand and jumping in the waves. It is a great place to relax, read, and even write a working paper on the diningroom table. That is just what I have done on occasions when I took a couple of my old students there to work with me. We have never rented the house, but keep it for family vacations, and sometimes lend it to friends. It has proved to be a great pleasure to all of us, despite the fact that developers have inevitably invaded the island. But they cannot take away the ocean or the canal or the wildlife that seems as prosperous as ever, including even dolphins in the canal now and then.

As I read over this chapter, it occurred to me that much of the second half sounds like entries in a journal. I think that that is because, although my visits to other universities were very acceptable to me and were generously negotiated by good friends, they made little lasting impression on me. Perhaps that is because they generally were short. That is not true, however, of the story of my precious laboratory. I was passionately interested in it and in all the possibilities of research that could be carried on. Nevertheless, one's friends retire or move away, colleagues and department heads change, and new directions are inevitably emphasized. You are still a friend but no longer an insider. A passionate interest in your own laboratory may be looked on with kindly tolerance indeed, but eventually few new students are likely to be assigned to it.

12

Life After the Lab

Is there life after the lab? In 1987 I was about to find out. My daughter telephoned me from Middlebury one day and said, "The house two doors from us is for sale. You must buy it!" At first, I had no thought of moving, but contemplation of the future and several serious considerations moved me. Since my husband's death, I had been living all alone in a house intended for a family. I had two studies, four bedrooms, a double garage (with an upstairs), a very large yard to keep up, and an uphill half-circle driveway that had to be plowed when it snowed. Although I had my lab, my department had changed greatly. My good friend Ulric Neisser had moved to take a professorship at Emory University, the Smiths had moved to Bowling Green University, the Ryans had gone to a retirement village in Pennsylvania, and Robbie MacLeod had died. My graduate students had become my best friends, but of course they completed their degrees and moved away to jobs. It is worth remarking, though, that one's graduate students (and in my case, my husband's as well) become one's friends for life. They are younger than one's colleagues, so they are still there to be enjoyed as the circle of older friends dwindles, but few of them were in Ithaca. Maybe it was time for me to make a change.

I went to see the house in Middlebury. It was a brick house, all on one floor except for a large basement. From the back windows, there was a very fine view of the Green Mountains. Details of the house's arrangement were not to my taste, but they could be changed. We consulted an architect friend of my son-in-law, who practices in Hanover, New Hampshire, and he came up with an excellent plan: to enclose the side porch and merge it with a small back bedroom to make a very large, light study with plenty of bookcases built in. We would then add a small porch at the entrance, stretching around the side to a wide deck across the back, looking toward the mountains. That left me two bedrooms, a livingroom and dining room, and a kitchen to be renovated and given a skylight. There were two bathrooms, so the shower in one was sacrificed to install laundry equipment. No more basement laundry!

I decided to do it. There were no longer so many friends to leave behind, and I might be able to find some in the Psychology Department of Middlebury College. I sold my house in Ithaca (that was the easiest part of the move) and proceeded to divest excess furniture, books, and the assorted accumulation from living 30 years in one house. Jerry came from South Carolina with Michael, then a little boy of 10 years. We rented a big U-Haul truck, and we filled it with tables, chairs, desks, and bookcases. I still have a vivid mental picture of the truck rolling down my curved driveway, with Jerry and little Michael on the driver's bench headed for South Carolina. Lois was probably not too happy when the truck was unpacked and she had to find room for all its contents.

My new home in Middlebury was fitted with carpets in my study and the living and dining rooms, pretty linoleum in the kitchen and bathrooms, and all new appliances. I moved in with the pieces I had chosen to keep (including my great-grandparents' gilt-framed pier glass mirror). The result was very attractive and comfortable. Still, I missed Ithaca.

Christmas came and all my family arrived to celebrate and admire my new quarters. I had brought along the traditional tree ornaments, and a Christmas tree looked nice in front of the great pier glass. My sister stayed with me, and Jerry and Lois and their boys stayed in a bed and breakfast establishment down the street. With Jean close by, everything worked nicely.

But what would I do without any research projects to plan, carry out, and tease my brain? Years earlier I had a friend, John Stephens, whom we knew during the war years, who announced to me his retirement from Johns Hopkins University. When I next saw him, I asked, "But John, what are you going to do?" He answered, grinning, "From now on, I am just going to emit wisdom!" That was not exactly what I had in mind, but I did plan to write about ideas that I had been contemplating over the years of research, especially about the concepts of perceptual learning and development, which I considered peculiarly *my* topic. My 1969 book on perceptual learning had created a field where there actually was none before. I had performed many an experiment in the field, recently with infants as well as older children and adults, and I thought I would expand and exploit the ideas that had been accumulating.

But I did not begin at once. I did not even stay in my new home the spring after I moved. Ulric Neisser, my old friend, invited me to take his place at Emory University while he went on a semester's sabbatical leave. I was to give a seminar and keep an eye on his graduate students. The prospect of academe again and the nearness of Atlanta to Columbia, South Carolina, easily persuaded me. A small furnished house belonging to the University, quite near the campus, was available, and I was to use Dick Neisser's very large, fine office. There were pleasant colleagues, and good graduate students attended my seminar. I made friends with them all, but there were two young, first-year graduate students who were to become my special friends, Karen Adolph and Marion Eppler. They were attracted by ideas that I presented in my seminar, such as my husband's concept of affordance, and they both had decided on developmental psychology as their major field for research and teaching. Both needed, in the course of that semester, to find a problem on which they could begin to focus their research. Needless to say, this was an endeavor that I was pleased to help with.

Karen had had some experience in a nursery school and was attracted by children's playground activities, especially motor ones like using the playground equipment. Now she wanted to look at it from a psychologist's standpoint. She narrowed her ideas down to using a sliding board, and then finally to looking at spontaneous exploratory behavior when beginning the pursuit. But a more specific question was needed. I was interested in exploration of surfaces in new situations, and we finally settled on presenting several surfaces, all sloping downward from a central pedestal, to see if young children would test them out for the affordance of "slideability" and choose the one that offered most. One surface was to be carpeted (safe, but not very "slideable"), one smooth and relatively slippery, and the third something rather neutral. This was not a very focused question, but the thing was to get started and then sharpen it up. There was a serious problem of where to put the large piece of apparatus that was being designed and built. No small research spaces reserved for first year-graduate students would do. We had an inspiration—why not Dick Neisser's large, commodious office? We moved things around and the new contraption of assorted sliding boards was moved in. A bevy of 2-year-olds was tried out.

No great discoveries were made at this point, but Karen got started, soon began asking more pointed questions, and eventually, became the world's expert on how infants learn to progress downhill (Adolph, 1997). Neisser's surprise at the transformation of his office when he returned was complete! Marion's problem was not so unwieldy; she eventually worked on the effect of a developing action system on exploratory behavior (Eppler, 1995).

Despite my role in devastating his office, Neisser invited me back again for the spring term of each of 2 following years, to my pleasure. I could continue my advising of the two young women, who are now my close friends. One other visit followed directly from this new contact. Karen felt the need to increase her knowledge of motor systems and to learn about a new trend called dynamic systems development. Dr. Esther Thelen at Indiana University, an expert in the area, was appealed to, and she invited Karen to spend the fall semester of 1989 with her. Indiana University has a Center for Advanced Study, and she invited me, too, to come and spend a month or two there. I did, to my profit and pleasure. Esther became a good friend and of course contributed greatly to Karen's graduate education.

The fall before this I spent away from Middlebury, too. Two of the most enthusiastic psychologists converted to my husband's ecological approach, Dr. Michael Turvey and Dr. Claudia Carillo, faculty members at the University of Connecticut, had started a research Center for Ecological Psychology there. How could I say no when they invited me there for the fall of 1988?

Meanwhile, Middlebury did become my home, of course. Summers, late springs, and early falls there are unsurpassed in their beauty, and I gradually became attached to my new home, especially my wonderful study. The winters were harsh and very snowy, however, and after a few years I began spending part of each winter in Columbia, South Carolina, with Jerry and Lois and their two sons. I usually went after Christmas, and I rapidly became acquainted with members of the Psychology Department at the university there. They offered me an office at the university to use during my stay, and I gladly accepted. Here was the chance to make progress on the writing I had planned, attend weekly colloquia, and make new friends among my colleagues. I wrote one of my best papers there, for the *Annual Review of Psychology*. I called it "Exploratory Behavior in the Development of Perceiving, Acting and the Acquiring of Knowledge" (E. J. Gibson, 1988). This topic was not regularly treated by the *Annual Reviews*. I was allowed to choose my topic, so I chose one that I considered important for understanding the origins of knowledge in infancy. I wrote:

Cognition, I suggest, rests on a foundation of knowledge acquired as a result of early exploration of events, people and things. As the baby's perceptual systems develop, exploratory activities are used to greater and greater advantage to discover the affordances that are pertinent to each phase of development. As new action systems mature, new affordances open up and new "experiments on the world" can be undertaken, with consequences to be observed. (E. J. Gibson, 1988, p. 3)

I emphasized the extreme importance of perceptual learning of this kind in the normal development of an infant; a kind of spontaneous information seeking propelled by the interaction of exploratory activity and events in the surrounding environment.

A little later, the MIT Press offered me the opportunity of putting together in one volume many of the experimental and theoretical papers of previous years. I called the book An Odyssey in Learning and Perception (E. J. Gibson, 1991). Besides including many reprinted papers, I wrote new text to go with them, explaining what motivated them at the time, what controversies they may have provoked or contributed to, and where they led eventually. The book came out in 1991, all 638 pages of it.

I wrote several papers by invitation, for special occasions, one a conference in 1994 organized by Cathy Dent-Read and Patricia Zukow-Goldring. The conference papers were eventually published in a book, Evolving Explanations of Development: Ecological Approaches to Organism-Environment Systems (Dent-Read & Zukow-Goldring, 1997). Of course I wrote about perceptual development, in a paper entitled "An Ecological Psychologist's Prolegomena for Perceptual Development: A Functional Approach" (E. J. Gibson, 1997). This paper is a kind of summary statement of my ecological view of how perception develops, with strong emphasis on a theory of perceptual learning. I have explained the theory in much greater detail and much better, I hope, in the book recently published on the topic by Anne Pick and myself (E. J. Gibson & Pick, 2000).

I mention one other conference that I attended in order to describe a rather amusing incident. For many years, the University of Minnesota has been the host for a symposium on human development, with invited speakers. In 1988, the topic was cognitive development. Elizabeth Spelke was a major speaker, and her title was "Where Perceiving Ends and Thinking Begins: The Apprehension of Objects in Infancy." There were two commentators on her paper, myself and Phillip Kellman, her own one-time graduate student. Both of us objected rather vociferously to what we considered a pro-innateness or nativistic tone in her discussion of very early object perception. She rose when we had finished, and replied, "Now I know how parents feel when the grandparents and grandchildren gang up against them!" I had been her mentor, as she had been Kellman's.

I have written several papers with Karen Adolph and Marion Eppler in recent years. On two or three occasions during their spring vacations we have spent a week together at the Gibson beach house on Fripp Island. Besides enjoying the time together, we usually collaborated on a paper or article, mostly on the topic of affordance; for example, a chapter written for *Advances in Infancy Research* called "Development of Perception of Affordances" (Adolph, Eppler, & Gibson, 1993). We meet when we can, recently at Karen's wedding to Peter Gordon (another psychologist). Marion, now on the faculty of East Carolina University, sometimes visits me in Columbia. Karen, with her husband and new baby, spent a recent Christmas vacation in my house in Vermont (empty because I spend Christmas now in Columbia).

Sometime in the 1990s I began thinking about revising my 1969 book on perceptual learning. It would have to be a very complete revision, because my ideas had changed over the years so as to complement my husband's ecological approach, not available when I wrote the 1969 book. The ecological approach and my ideas about how perception develops are extremely compatible, and I thought the new version might be valuable. I discussed the project with Anne Pick, my old student and very good friend, who said, "You must do it!" I asked if she would do it with me and be co-author. She readily agreed. We worked on the book for nearly 5 years, dividing up the chapters, criticizing and revising each other. I had been convinced for some time that the best opportunity for studying perceptual learning must be during the earliest period of development in the first 2 years, when language is not available, or only beginning to be, and when action systems are maturing. Studying learning in the course of early development is truly revealing and my expectations have paid off. Furthermore, a wealth of new research on perceptual development in infancy is available now, and it has proved to fit with our approach remarkably well. In recent years, published research on what infants perceive has frequently been relevant to ecological concerns, often centering on when an infant comes to perceive some environmental opportunity. What a surface affords, such as my own research on the visual cliff, is an example.

My work of the past decades has been rewarded with a number of honors, giving me great satisfaction and in several cases great pleasure. The most unexpected and exciting of these was receiving the National Medal of Science in 1992. There was a great celebration in Washington, DC, for the recipients, and all my family were invited. Jerry and Lois, with Michael (then 15), Jean and David with Elizabeth (also 15), and of course my sister all came. There was an elegant banquet the night before the award ceremony at the National Building Museum, a remarkable old building. It consists of an enormous empty atrium (filled with tables that evening), surrounded with tiers of balconies or galleries mounting up five stories. Dinner was elaborate, many courses and a different wine with each. The two teenagers climbed to the top gallery and waved to us gaily. Next morning was the presentation ceremony in the White House Rose Garden. I proudly include a photograph of President Bush handing me the medal. The medal is a very large gilt affair embossed with the figure of a man (of course) and it came in a leather case. There is also an elegant document to hang on the wall, which I did.

I was also the recipient of honorary degrees from several universities. It was especially pleasing to receive such an honor from institutions where I had served, as was the case with the University of South Carolina, Emory University, and Middlebury College. The president of the University of South Carolina was rumored to present gifts to the recipients, such as articles of Steuben glass. President Holderman did not give me a piece of Steuben glass, but he did give me a book by Pat Conroy, a fine novelist native to South Carolina. The book is at home and appreciated in our little library of local

Fig. 19. Eleanor Gibson receiving Medal of Science from President Bush in 1992.

documents at the beach house on Fripp Island. Unfortunately, it is inscribed to me by President Holderman, not by Pat Conroy. The commencement ceremony was memorable to me because I gave the address for the higher degree candidates, including Pearl Bailey. This was my only commencement address ever, and I was rather proud of it. Because it is short and still to the point, here it is:

> My first reaction to the invitation to speak to you today was surprise—I have spoken to many audiences, but never on an occasion like this. My second was to remember what I once heard a wise person say about commencement speeches: "You must either be very brilliant or very brief." I have chosen the second alternative. I remembered, too, my own commencement at Yale after graduate school. Like this occasion, only recipients of graduate degrees were present. We marched in cap and gown, under a very hot sun, led by a mace bearer and a band through the streets of New Haven to Woolsey Hall, observed by a few rather bored citizens. Once there, it took a seemingly interminable time to hand out all the diplomas. There was no speech. I don't remember even any congratulations. It was less than satisfying as a conclusion to a significant interval in our lives.

> Surely something commemorating the occasion should be said. After all those years of labor—four or more for many of you—ending perhaps in the trial by fire of the thesis defense, there must be some important comment to make to close that chapter of one's life.

> I know what is generally told undergraduates at their commencements. The speaker, whatever else the message may be, typically says, "Remember, your education isn't finished! You are only beginning!" But people who have made it to a graduate degree know that only too well. They *know* they'll never be through learning. Knowledge changes. One-time facts sometimes become fictions. New technologies arise and one must keep up with them. New and unforeseen problems arise. And one still has something to learn about "real life" when it comes to facing it in a profession. I had to learn about the status (more accurately, nonstatus) of women, first in the graduate schools of universities and then in jobs. That situation has changed for the better, but other trials are ahead. For those of you who plan to pursue an academic career, for example, you may already be steeling yourselves for the next ordeal, the battle for tenure and the struggle to swell the list of publications.

> But whatever the next hurdle you contemplate in your professional lives, some moments must be spared from it. Some for your personal lives, of course. Humanity begins at home. A desire for the comfort of a family—or whatever today's substitute for it is—is not merely selfish. I remember my mother-in-law saying, as I exhaustedly coped with my first baby, "Everybody should have one—it's very humanizing."

That's my point—we have to save some time for humanity in a broader sense, as well. You may wonder why someone should be saying this to you, in particular. There is a reason. When candidates are presented for a higher degree, it is always awarded with a reference to "all the privileges pertaining thereto." I wondered for many years just what one could expect by way of those privileges. Well, by this time I have found out. In every important sense, you have already had them.

How many people, even in our own privileged society, have the privilege of attending graduate school? We expect that all children in our society will attend school through the age of 16. Many drop out before finishing high school. I recently read in the annual report of the Carnegie Foundation for the Advancement of Teaching that in 1984 over half the students in Chicago high schools failed to graduate. Of those who make it through high school only a percentage attends technical school or a 2-year community college. A lesser percentage attends a 4-year college and actually achieves a bachelor's degree. And that's it for most people. According to a recent book on The Undergraduate Experience in America, the number of students going on to a doctoral degree from the so-called "Big 10" universities was 4 percent. For the small colleges of the country, the number would be far smaller. The picture presents a kind of hierarchy, a big tree diagram. On one side, all the branches contain more and more drop-outs and people whose formal education has been concluded. On the other, the branches, as they continue to fan out, contain fewer and fewer members, who are becoming ever more specialized in their own little branches.

For this rare chance of becoming specialists, we owe society something. What it is is different for every generation, and perhaps a little different for each one of us. But one thing is certain. Among you are the people who are going to do the teaching, guide the universities, pursue research, protect the rights of the less privileged in legislatures and courtrooms, heal the sick, and make decisions about life and death—in short, protect humanity in our society. That's a sobering thought.

What are the crying issues now, where humanity is fighting for its life? In my day, it was fascism and the ugly threats it brought. Every generation has its charge; and every one of you will have her or his own list. I have three issues that I consider of crisis proportions. The first, on all your lists too, I am sure, is the threat of nuclear holocaust. This one is so ubiquitous and its urgency so obvious, that I need fill it in no further. I assume that none of us wants humanity wiped out.

The second carries us back in history to the middle ages—who would have thought we should experience the threat of a black plague in the 20th century? In an article on AIDS, Stephen Jay Gould, today's most eminent evolutionary biologist, said:

The evolutionary perspective is correct, but utterly inappropriate for our *human* scale. Yes, AIDS is a natural phenomenon, one of a recurring class of pandemic diseases. Yes, AIDS may run through the entire population, and may carry off a quarter or more of us. Yes, it may make no *biological* difference to Homo sapiens in the long run: there will still be plenty of us left and we can start again. Evolution cares as little for its agents—organisms struggling for reproductive success—as physics cares for individual atoms of hydrogen in the sun. But we care. These atoms are our neighbors, our lovers, our children and ourselves. AIDS is both a natural phenomenon and, potentially, the greatest natural tragedy in human history.

Gould speaks for us all in this paragraph. He doesn't tell us what to do. We are the people who are supposed to be able to figure that out.

My third issue may seem to you less critical, as it certainly is less flamboyant. But it is insidious, a creeping danger that could (and I am afraid may) totally undermine our society. One way to put it is the threat of national self-indulgence, to such an extent that our whole social structure could fall under debt, bankruptcy, and an ominous trend to greater inequality (enrichment of some at the cost of the impoverishment of others).[1] This third issue worries me the most of the three, because as an educator I see it reflected in the ambitions of bright young people. It is not just the national debt, though that seems to mirror the greed and the "thinking big" of the last decade. A congressman (maybe several of them) recently said, "The party's over. People are about to discover that 'reality is reality.'" But the problem is not one that will be solved by passing a law or raising taxes. The cause goes deeper; it has become rooted in people's attitudes.

It used to be that the brightest and best of a college's seniors had a "calling," a vocation. Some wanted to teach the young; some wanted to join the Peace Corps to bring better health and education to less fortunate parts of the world; some wanted to dedicate their lives to research, or heal the sick. But over the last decade, these motives have become scarcer and scarcer in the young people I have talked to. The main motive seems to be to "make a buck"—or rather, megabucks. We seem to be living in a hard-edged, competitive society. There were 13 times as many MBAs in 1984 as in 1960. One director of a college placement office said, "Our students are interested in making money, being successful, and finding a job with a Fortune 500 company." That may not be bad in itself, but when it becomes an *end* in itself it is frightening.

What can we do to restore some feeling of commitment to *humanity* in the young, particularly? I do not know, but I think it is gong to be your problem, as the threat of fascism was my generation's. How do we make education an ex-

---

[1]According to the Joint Economic Committee of Congress, "Just 1% of Americans now own more than a third of total wealth." (Poverty amidst plenty.)

perience that leads students to seek ideals and loyalties beyond their personal ones? To value *integrity* in scholarship, in science, in business, and in law? A part of the answer is that you yourselves, the people who have enjoyed the most that society has to offer in an excellent education, must constitute the models.

Now, have I nothing optimistic to say? Do the privileges you have enjoyed confer upon you nothing but obligations? By all means; there is something to say on the other side. Whatever its responsibilities and duties, the life of an educated person is the richest and best. The world has been opened up for you to find and enjoy its true riches. You have won the rewards that education brings, and are entitled to enjoy them, however grim society's problems.

Some of you will make discoveries, or create something new—a picture, a great building, a beautiful park, perhaps. Few of us have that satisfaction, but we all can find satisfaction in a helping role, and joy in understanding science, listening to music, looking at beautiful things, and reading about the things we would like to understand. That is what you have won. Clark Seelye, the first president of Smith, my old college, described your prize thus:

> "A well-educated mind is the most useful of all possessions and next to a sound heart the most valuable. For the merchandise of it is better than silver, and the gain thereof better than fine gold."

I am not a very religious person, but I conclude with a verse from the Bible that seems right for this important occasion: "Finally, Brethren, whatsoever things are just, whatsoever things are true, whatsoever things are honest, whatsoever things are pure, whatsoever things are lovely—if there be any virtue, if there be any praise, think on these things."

Congratulations and good wishes.

In 1996, I was the recipient of an honorary degree from Yale University. Yale had presented me with their Wilbur Cross Medal in 1973. I suspect that it is intended as an award for their old PhDs who have turned out satisfactorily. The honorary doctorate was a real surprise. I was to invite as many guests as I wished for the celebration. My daughter Jean and son-in-law David accompanied me to New Haven. The precommencement dinner was held at the president's house and my Yale friends Neal and Marion Miller and Carol Fowler joined us. It was a delightful occasion, not too formal. The Whiffenpoofs came to sing to us, standing on the large hall staircase. The president ran to the stairs and stood with them, calling out, "anyone who wants to sing, come join us." Paul Simon, the singer, also an honorary degree recipient, joined them. The next day was fine, and more psychologist friends came to the postcommencement luncheon. I rather wished, meanly, that

Professor Yerkes, who had treated me so summarily, could have known about my eventual triumph! But I wished even more that Professor Hull, who had been a kind and helpful mentor, had known. He'd have been proud of his old student, I think.

My travels since then have been few, because of deteriorating health. I have had a dickey heart since I was 11 years old and was ill with rheumatic fever. It didn't stop me from doing most things, even though it was coupled with high blood pressure. But about 10 years ago, my cardiologist began threatening me with the necessity of valve surgery, and in 1995, he insisted that it couldn't wait any longer. So, I had open heart surgery and my aortic valve was replaced. Somehow, during the surgical procedure, an inexperienced anesthetist injured my vocal cords, to their eternal impairment. To make things worse, I came down with pneumonia a couple of weeks later. Two years after that, I succumbed to pneumonia again, not improving my heart condition. The consequence is that my travels now are pretty much confined to my trips to South Carolina and back to Vermont. But I can rejoice in the fact that I have loving family in both places, with help when I need it. In addition, I can still write, and I do. Sometimes I have assigned work to do, such as journal articles to review or a chapter to contribute to a book or a symposium; sometimes I write on my own or with a friend, like the book with Anne Pick. The real catastrophe would be, as my philosopher friend Marjorie Grene reminds me, to run out of work. It's what we do, and need to do.

I have been helped, too, by finding a new group of friends. They are, literally, Friends. The heavy dose of Calvinism that my husband and I were both given in childhood had left us with no wish to embrace religion. We had simply left it alone and left our children to find out about it for themselves, if they ever wanted to. As it happened, our daughter Jean did. Whether it was the influence of her Grandmother Gibson or of Northfield, her school, I don't know. It was spontaneous, in any case, and she went searching for what she needed. Her discovery was the Society of Friends, when she was in graduate school at Cornell. She joined the group there and has been a very loyal and devoted Friend since, serving on the American Friends Service Committee (AFSC), going to quarterly meetings, and working in their tradition. There is a Middlebury Friends meeting, and after moving to Middlebury I began to attend it, after a while becoming a regular. The silent worship and the wonderful support of all the group are irreplaceable in my life now.

All this time I have missed my husband very much, especially as my life has become more isolated. Still, I can take great satisfaction in the testimonials to his memory, which are many. The successful and growing International Society for Ecological Psychology with its journal and annual meetings is one of them. Equally important are the translations of his books. His last book, *The Ecological Approach to Visual Perception*, has been translated into French, Russian, Chinese, Japanese, and Italian (twice). It has not been translated into German, so far as I know. I hope that is because all the psychologists in that country read English. It was good to see, too, that two new encyclopedias, one of cognitive science and one of psychology, include major articles on his life and work. It is good, too, that my Gibson grandsons have both taken psychology courses in college and took pleasure in finding their grandparents' names in their textbooks.

Finally, what are we to think about the scene in experimental psychology today? I am not entirely happy about it, as my readers may detect. Some psychology departments have changed their names to "Department of Cognitive Science" or even "Department of Cognitive Neuroscience." Prizes are going to psychologists who study neuroscience in relation to thinking or consciousness. There is certainly nothing wrong with studying thinking and neural processes, but I am not sure that the combination is going anywhere and I am sorry to see fashion desert the study of behavior, which I still consider the important subject matter for a psychologist. Another trend is an emphasis—overemphasis, I believe—on the role of genes in development of perception and cognition. I think development is driven by many other factors as well, all interacting, and I want to see more emphasis on learning, especially in early life. A third trend I can heartily applaud: Research on perceptual development in infants has increased many fold in the last decade and a half. It is not research on discriminating pure colors or sounds or pictured geometrical forms; it focuses on the development of perception of valuable information like human speech and useful properties of the world. It all fits beautifully with an ecological approach to perception and perceptual development. Anne Pick and I have made the most of it in our book, *An Ecological Approach to Perceptual Learning and Development* (E. J. Gibson & Pick, 2000), providing a happy ending for me.

Postscript

I am told by my son that I should return now to the subject of our forbears, as described in my first chapter, and show how their stern Protestant grit and fortitude made our two lives what they were. In this period of the fashionable gene should we be able to find an explanation of it all in the heritage that they gave us? Where among these sturdy Presbyterians, independent, ambitious, and self-disciplined farmers and businessmen, do we find the material that created two academics, scientists and scholars both? I don't believe that genetic inheritance is the only place to look in seeking to understand the development of individuals. Many factors play a role in a complex interaction, my own research tells me.

What our staunch Presbyterian families gave us was discipline, a fine education, and strong support for engaging in the field of endeavor that we chose (it could just as well have been law or medicine or business). What else was important then? The environments that each of us chose, the opportunities that they offered, even fortuitous happenings. If James had not taken Langfeldt's course in advanced experimental psychology his senior year at Princeton, and if Professor Langfeldt had not offered him a graduate assistantship, he might not have been a psychologist. If it had not rained the day of the senior garden party at Smith in 1930, I might not have been! We act on our affordances and these play a large role in determining not only our life histories but the kind of people we become. The dynamics of our relationships with other persons is equally important.

The dynamics of the relationship between my husband and myself seems to me now to have been a powerfully determining factor in whatever heights of achievement we may have attained. We respected one another's intelligence, creativity, and determination, and were mutually interested in each other's project or pet theory of the moment. We argued, always, over the meaning of any new developments, and when we reached an agreement, the result was usually good and our satisfaction great. There was never any question about our sharing goals, or of making some temporary sacrifice for the progress of them. I don't detect any particular genes in this mixture, rather an interaction of genes with the personal attraction of two people, their background, talents, interests, and opportunities. The single most important factor for me was my complete trust in the integrity of my husband's thinking. Perhaps integrity was what his forebears bequeathed him.

I thought I had said it all, at this point, until an old graduate student, Karen Adolph, came to visit me with her baby, the happiest of women. She read these memoirs and put the manuscript down, looking unhappy. I asked, "What's wrong, Karen? Don't you like my story?" She said, "No. It's too sad." I gathered after a while that she enjoyed the beginning and the central chapters where new jobs and babies and successful publications and travel were the themes, but then she found the later chapters depressing.

I wondered if I had failed by omitting many of the pains that did come in earlier years, like those nights when I sat up holding the hands of sobbing children as we waited for the morning and the doctor to come to attend to the infected ear. Or the terrible train trip from Texas to California in 1943 with an injured child and a 3-month-old baby. This took 3 days in the heat with no diaper disposal and almost unsolveable problems in feeding the children (Jerry couldn't walk to the dining car and Jean needed warmed bottles of fresh formula). Then there was the time we were told that we had 1 week to move from the wartime rented house in Santa Ana—but where? The Army Emergency Relief found us a place in the nick of time, but what a misery! Home again, at last, was better. Finding time for research was hard, so we had to leave Smith, much as we loved it and our house there. But we soon came to love Cornell, too, so it was no tragedy. Getting lab space was difficult at Cornell, and there was the fact that I spent more than 15 years there with no lab of my own and no place on the university faculty—just a lowly research associate. During his 40s, my husband gradually lost his hearing, a terrible, terrible deprivation. I'll stop my depressing list right there.

But neither was later life all gloom and doom. My husband's research continued and his ideas, always creative, reached genius level. His students adored him. The university in the end gave me a Susan Linn Sage Professorship and a lab of my own. Karen, however, was no doubt thinking of the sadness of my life without Jimmy, recounted in the last two chapters. It was sad. I never found a companion who could replace him, even after 20 years. But there have been compensations. Karen herself, along with Marion Eppler, my last two graduate students, are among them. It is amazing how important one's students become. They remain one's friends for life. Christmas cards, notices of babies, and reprints pour in.

I tell a last story about one of my old graduate students, Pat Cabe. Pat teaches at the University of North Carolina at Pembroke. It is not too far from Columbia, South Carolina, where I spend my winters. On a recent occasion, I had just spent a long day working on the index of my last book (E. J. Gibson & Pick, 2000). Fortunately, I had some help. A nice graduate student in social work spent some time with me during the day, and I discovered she was a whiz on the computer. She worked on the index with me and saved me much trouble. It was 5:30 p. m. that day when the doorbell rang and there was Pat Cabe. He had been giving a talk at a nearby college and thought he would stop for a minute on his way home. I told him about working on the index and my good fortune in having this student to ease the labor. "Oh, I'll never forget the labor of making an index," he said. "All those hundreds of 3 by 5 cards and worrying over where they all belonged." I evidently looked a little puzzled, for Pat then said, "Don't you remember? I did the index for you on your 1969 book." That was more than 600 pages long, and I had forgotten Pat's labors!

A few days later, I received an e-mail message from Pat, containing a long list of my husband's and my one-time graduate students. They weren't all there, but there were many I had forgotten. He even knew where they were now, in most cases. That is good, because we like to let them know where the meetings of the Society for Ecological Psychology will be, often in Canada or Europe. More recently, I received a book in the mail from Roberta Golinkoff, an old graduate student—a marvelous book called How Babies Talk. She has a named professorship now, and most all of our former students are full professors.

There are other rewards besides the graduate students—the material ones, of course, like honorary degrees—but they really don't count much. Old friends do. My old friend Marjorie Grene, an academic if I ever knew one, is exactly my age and wonderful fun. She never stops working; she still teaches and lectures in 3 languages, and counsels me from time to time on the importance of work. She's right.

I wind up with the greatest reward and pleasure of all—my family, of course. My two perfect children, Jerry and Jean Gibson, married two per-fect mates, Lois Rauch and David Rosenberg, both as kind and loving to me as my own children. Both pairs of them produced two wonderful children, Eli and Elizabeth Rosenberg and Michael and Jonathan Gibson. Two of the boys and Elizabeth have finished college, all having distinguished them-selves, and Jonathan, the youngest, is doing us proud at Duke. These are not matters that make for sadness.

I did not intend my last two chapters to sound sad. Some of life is sad, by its very nature. Adolescence has always seemed miserable to me, but life opens up as an adventure, full of questions, after that. It is ours to make what we can of it. It's not the same for any two people, but that's what life is like. Every day brings new affordances. Perceiving them makes all the difference, espe-cially when there is more than one that could be acted upon, so choices must be made. Which choice will afford the most opportunities and satisfaction? This book is about how two of us managed this challenge together.

References

Adolph, K. E. (1997). Learning in the development of infant locomotion. *Monographs of the Society for Research in Child Development;62*(3, Serial No. 251).

Adolph, K. E., Eppler, M. A., & Gibson, E. J. (1993). Development of perception of affordances. In C. Rovee-Collier & L. P. Lipsitt (Eds.), *Advances in infancy research* (Vol. 8, pp. 51–98). Norwood, NJ: Ablex.

Benjamin, L. T., Jr. (1977). The psychological round table: Revolution of 1936. *American Psychologist, 32*, 542–549.

Boring, E. G. (1933). *The physical dimensions of consciousness*. New York: Century.

Boring, E. G. (1938). The Society of Experimental Psychologists: 1904–1938. *American Journal of Psychology, 51*, 410–423.

Boring, E. G. (1951). Review of J. J. Gibson's *Perception of the visual world*. *Psychological Bulletin, 48*, 360–363.

Boring, E. G. (1952). Visual perception as invariance. *Psychological Review, 59*, 141–148.

Boring, E. G. (1953). The Gibsonian visual field. *Psychological Review, 59*, 246–247.

Boring, E. G. (1967). Titchener's experimentalists. *Journal of the History of the Behavioral Sciences, 3*, 315–325.

Bower, T. G. R. (1965). Stimulus variables determining space perception in infants. *Science, 149*, 88–89.

Bower, T. G. R. (1966). Slant perception and shape constancy in infants. *Science, 151,* 832–834.

Carmichael, L. (1950). Introduction. In J. J. Gibson, *The perception of the visual world* (pp. v–vi). Cambridge, MA: Riverside.

Dent-Read, C., & Zukow-Goldring, P. (Eds.) (1997). *Evolving explanations of development: Ecological approaches to organism–environment systems.* Washington, DC: American Psychological Association.

Eppler, M. A. (1995). Development of manipulatory skills and the deployment of attention. *Infant Behavior and Development, 18,* 391–405.

Furumoto, L. (1998). Lucy May Boring (1886–1996). *American Psychologist, 53,* 59.

Garner, W. R. (1970). Processing sensory information. *Science, 168,* 958–959.

Gibson, E. J. (1939). Sensory generalization with voluntary reactions. *Journal of Experimental Psychology, 24,* 237–253.

Gibson, E. J. (1940). A systematic application of the concepts of generalization and differentiation to verbal learning. *Psychological Review, 47,* 196–229.

Gibson, E. J. (1941) Retroactive inhibition as a function of degree of generalization between tasks. *Journal of Experimental Psychology, 28,* 93–115.

Gibson, E. J. (1942). Intra-list generalization as a factor in verbal learning. *Journal of Experimental Psychology, 30,* 185–200.

Gibson, E. J. (1965). Learning to read. *Science, 148,* 1066–1072.

Gibson, E. J. (1969). *Principles of perceptual learning and development.* New York: Appleton-Century-Crofts.

Gibson, E. J. (1970a). The development of perception as an active process. *American Scientist, 58,* 98–107.

Gibson, E. J. (1970b). The ontogeny of reading. *American Psychologist, 25,* 136–140.

Gibson, E. J. (1988). Exploratory behavior in the development of perceiving, acting, and the acquiring of knowledge. *Annual Review of Psychology, 39,* 1–41.

Gibson, E. J. (1991). *Odyssey in learning and perception.* Cambridge, MA: MIT Press.

Gibson, E. J. (1997). An ecological psychologist's prologomena for perceptual development: A functional approach. In C. Dent-Read & Zukow-Goldring (Eds.), *Evolving explanations of development* (pp. 23–45). Washingon, DC: American Psychological Association.

Gibson, E. J. & Gibson, J. J. (1972, June 23). The senses as information-seeking systems. *The London Times Literary Supplement,* 711–712.

Gibson, E. J., Gibson, J. J., Pick, A. D., & Osser, H. (1962). A developmental study of the discrimination of letter-like forms. *Journal of Comparative and Physiological Psychology, 55,* 897–906.

Gibson, E. J., & Levin, H. (1975). *The psychology of reading.* Cambridge, MA: MIT Press.

Gibson, E. J., Owsley, C. J., & Johnston, J. (1978). Perception of invariants by five-month-old infants: Differentiation of two types of motion. *Developmental Psychology, 14,* 407–415.

Gibson, E. J., & Pick, A.D. (2000). *Perceptual learning and development: An ecological approach*. New York: Oxford University Press.

Gibson, E. J., Riccio, G., Rosenberg, D., Schmuckler, M. A., Stoffregen, T. A., & Taormina, J. (1987). Detection of the traversability of surfaces by crawling and walking infants. *Journal of Experimental Psychology: Perception and Performance, 13*, 533–544.

Gibson, E. J., & Schmuckler, M. A. (1989). Going somewhere: An ecological and experimental approach to development of mobility. *Ecological Psychology, 1*, 3–25

Gibson, E. J., & Walk, R. D. (1956). The effect of prolonged exposure to visually presented patterns on learning to discriminate them. *Journal of Comparative and Physiological Psychology, 49*, 239–242.

Gibson, E. J., & Walk, R. D. (1960). The "visual cliff." *Scientific American, 202*, 64–71.

Gibson, E. J., Walk, R.D., & Tighe, T. J. (1959). Enhancement and deprivation of visual stimulation during rearing as factors in visual discrimination learning. *Journal of Comparative and Physiological Psychology, 52*, 74–81.

Gibson, E. J., & Walker, A. (1984). Development of knowledge of visual and tactual affordance of substance. *Child Development, 55*, 453–460.

Gibson, J. J., (1933). Adaptation, after-effect and contrast in the perception of curved lines. *Journal of Experimental Psychology, 16*, 1–31.

Gibson, J. J. (1935). Studies in psychology from Smith College. *Psychological Monographs, 46*(6, No. 210).

Gibson, J. J. (1947). *Motion picture testing and research* (Report No. 7, Army Air Forces Aviation Psychology Program Research Reports). Washington DC: U. S. Government Printing Office.

Gibson, J. J. (1950). *The perception of the visual world*. Cambridge, MA: Riverside.

Gibson, J. J. (1952). The visual field and the visual world: A reply to Professor Boring. *Psychological Review, 59*, 149–151.

Gibson, J. J. (1958). Visually controlled locomotion and visual orientation in animals and man. *British Journal of Psychology, 49*, 182–194.

Gibson, J. J. (1966). *The senses considered as perceptual systems*. Boston, MA: Houghton-Mifflin.

Gibson, J. J. (1967). Autobiography. In E. G. Boring & G. Lindsey (Eds.), *A history of psychology in autobiography* (Vol.5 pp. 125–143). New York: Appleton-Century-Crofts.

Gibson, J. J. (1979a). *The ecological approach to visual perception*. Boston: Houghton-Mifflin.

Gibson, J. J. (1979b). Foreword. In A. D. Pick (Ed.), *Perception and its development* (pp. ix–xiii). Hillsdale, NJ: Lawrence Erlbaum Associates.

Gibson, J. J. & Carel, W. (1952). Does motion perspective independently produce the impression of a receding surface? *Journal of Experimental Psychology, 44*, 16–18.

Gibson, J. J., & Crooks, L. E. (1938). A theoretical field-analysis of automobile-driving. *American Journal of Psychology, 51*, 453–471.

Gibson, J. J., & Gibson, E. J. (1955a). Perceptual learning: Differentiation or enrichment? *Psychological Review, 62,* 32–41.

Gibson, J. J., & Gibson, E. J. (1955b). What is learned in perceptual learning? A reply to Professor Postman. *Psychological Review, 62,* 447–450.

Gibson, J. J., & Gibson, E. J. (1957). Continuous perspective transformations and the perception of rigid motion. *Journal of Experimental Psychology, 54,* 129–138.

Gibson, J. J., Olum, P., & Rosenblatt, F. (1955). Parallax and perspective during aircraft landings. *American Journal of Psychology, 68,* 372–385.

Hay, J. C., & Pick, H. L., Jr. (1966). Gaze-contingent adaptation and prism orientation. *Journal of Experimental Psychology, 72,* 640–648.

Hebb, D. O. (1937). The innate organization of visual activity: I. Perception of figures by rats reared in total darkness. *Journal of Genetic Psychology, 51,* 101–126.

Heider, F. (1955). The life of a psychologist, an autobiography. Lawrence: University Press of Kansas.

Hochberg, J. (1957). The effects of the Gestalt revolution in psychology. *Psychological Review, 64,* 73–84.

Hochberg, J. (1990). After the revolution. *Contemporary Psychology, 35,* 750–752.

Holt, E. B. (1915), *The Freudian wish and its place in ethics.* New York: Holt.

Holt, E. B. (1931). *Animal drive and the learning process: An essay toward radical empiricism.* New York: Holt.

Hull, C. L. (1929). A functional interpretation of the conditioned reflex. *Psychological Review, 36,* 498–511.

Hull, C. L. (1932). The goal gradient hypothesis and maze learning. *Psychological Review, 39,* 25–43.

Hull, C. L. (1934). The concept of the habit-family hierarchy and maze learning. *Psychological Review, 41,* 33–52, 134–152.

Johansson, G. (1950). *Configurations in event perception.* Uppsala, Sweden: Almquist & Wiksell.

Kellman, P. J., Gleitman, H., & Spelke, E. S. (1987). Object and observer motion in the perception of objects by infants. *Journal of Experimental Psychology: Human Performance and Perception. 13,* 586–593.

Kohler, I. (1964). The formation and transformation of the perceptual world. *Psychological Issues* (Vol. III, No. 4). New York: International Universities Press.

Lashley, K. S., & Russell, J. T. (1934). The mechanism of vision: XI. A preliminary test of innate organization. *Journal of Genetic Psychology, 45,* 136–144.

Lee, D. N. (1976). A theory of visual control of braking based on information about time-to-collision. *Perception, 5,* 437–459.

Lee, D. N., & Aronson, E. (1974). Visual proprioceptive control of standing in human infants. *Perception and Psychophysics, 15,* 529–532.

Lombardo, T. J. (1987). *The reciprocity of perceiver and environment: The evolution of James J. Gibson's ecological psychology.* Hillsdale, N J: Lawrence Erlbaum Associates.

MacLeod, R. B., & Pick, H. L. (Eds.) (1974). *Perception: Essays in Honor of James J. Gibson*. Ithaca, NY: Cornell University Press.

Neisser, U. (1988). Five kinds of self-knowledge. *Philosophical Psychology, 1*, 35–59.

Pick, A. D. (Ed.). (1979). *Perception and its Development*. Hillsdale, N J: Lawrence Erlbaum, Associates.

Pick, H. L., & Hay, J. C. (1966). Gaze-contingent adaptation to prismatic spectacles. *American Journal of Psychology, 79*, 443–450.

Pittenger, J., Reed, E., Kim, M., & Best, L. (Eds.). (1997). The purple perils: A selection of James J. Gibson's unpublished essays on the psychology of perception. [on-line]. Retrieved December 29, 2000 from the World Wide Web: http://lor.trincoll.edu/~psyc/perils.

Postman, L. (1955). Association theory and perceptual learning. *Psychological Review, 62*, 438–446.

Reed, E. (1988). *James J. Gibson and the psychology of perception*. New Haven, CT: Yale University Press.

Reed, E., & Jones, R. (1982). *Reasons for realism: Selected essays of James J. Gibson*. Hillsdale, N J: Lawrence Erlbaum Associates.

Restle, F. (1980). The seer of Ithaca. *Contemporary Psychology, 25*, 291–293.

Spelke, E. S. (1976). Infants' intermodal perception of events. *Cognitive Psychology, 8*, 553–560.

Stoffregen, T. A., Schmuckler, M. A., & Gibson, E. J. (1987). Use of central and peripheral optical flow in stance and locomotion in young walkers. *Perception, 16*, 113–119.

von Hofsten, C. (1980). Predictive reaching for moving objects by human infants. *Journal of Experimental Child Psychology, 30*, 369–382.

von Hofsten, C. (1993). Prospective control: A basic aspect of action development. *Human Development, 36*, 253–270.

Walk, R. D., Gibson, E. J., & Tighe, T. J. (1957). Behavior of light-and dark-reared rats on a visual cliff. *Science, 126*, 80-81.

Woodworth, R. S. (1938). *Experimental psychology*. New York: Holt.

Yonas, A., & Gibson, E. J. (1967 April). *A developmental study of feature-processing strategies in letter discrimination*. Paper presented at the Eastern Psychological Association, Boston.

Index